About Island Press

Since 1984, the nonprofit Island Press has been stimulating, shaping, and communicating the ideas that are essential for solving environmental problems worldwide. With more than 800 titles in print and some 40 new releases each year, we are the nation's leading publisher on environmental issues. We identify innovative thinkers and emerging trends in the environmental field. We work with world-renowned experts and authors to develop cross-disciplinary solutions to environmental challenges.

Island Press designs and implements coordinated book publication campaigns in order to communicate our critical messages in print, in person, and online using the latest technologies, programs, and the media. Our goal: to reach targeted audiences—scientists, policymakers, environmental advocates, the media, and concerned citizens—who can and will take action to protect the plants and animals that enrich our world, the ecosystems we need to survive, the water we drink, and the air we breathe.

Island Press gratefully acknowledges the support of its work by the Agua Fund, Inc., Annenberg Foundation, The Christensen Fund, The Nathan Cummings Foundation, The Geraldine R. Dodge Foundation, Doris Duke Charitable Foundation, The Educational Foundation of America, Betsy and Jesse Fink Foundation, The William and Flora Hewlett Foundation, The Kendeda Fund, The Forrest and Frances Lattner Foundation, The Andrew W. Mellon Foundation, The Curtis and Edith Munson Foundation, Oak Foundation, The Overbrook Foundation, the David and Lucile Packard Foundation, The Summit Fund of Washington, Trust for Architectural Easements, Wallace Global Fund, The Winslow Foundation, and other generous donors.

The opinions expressed in this book are those of the author(s) and do not necessarily reflect the views of our donors.

RESILIENT CITIES

RESILIENT CITIES
RESPONDING TO PEAK OIL AND CLIMATE CHANGE

Peter Newman,
Timothy Beatley, and
Heather Boyer

ISLANDPRESS

Washington • Covelo • London

Newman, Peter, Dr.
    Resilient cities : responding to peak oil and climate change / by Peter Newman, Timothy Beatley, and Heather Boyer.
        p.   cm.
    Includes bibliographical references and index.
    ISBN-13: 978-1-59726-498-3 (hardcover : alk. paper)
    ISBN-10: 1-59726-498-9 (hardcover : alk. paper)
    ISBN-13: 978-1-59726-499-0 (pbk. : alk. paper)
    ISBN-10: 1-59726-499-7 (pbk. : alk. paper)
    1. Urban ecology. 2. City planning. 3. Sustainable development. I. Beatley, Timothy. II. Boyer, Heather. III. Title.
    HT241.N495 2008
    307.76—dc22
2008014874

Printed on recycled, acid-free paper ♲

Manufactured in the United States of America
10 9 8 7 6 5 4 3 2 1

Keywords: Urban planning, green architecture, climate change, urban policy, peak oil, energy policy, biofuels, resiliency, mass transit, automobile dependency, fossil fuel use, solar energy, wind energy, energy policy, housing affordability, equity, green infrastructure, global issues, environmental health

Contents

Preface

How did I get into Peak Oil and Climate Change?
Peter Newman

My involvement in these issues goes back to the first oil crisis in 1973 when I was a postdoctoral student at Stanford University in California. For the first time an external force had been imposed on the supply chain for gasoline. The OPEC-induced physical reductions in supply caused real panic in the community as people stayed at home or queued for hours for diminishing supplies. Social disarray began to be displayed as some people stole fuel, and across society there were myths about giant caverns of oil being stored by greedy oil companies and environmentalists were being accused of causing the decline. What stayed with me from this time was how suddenly a city can flip into a state of fear. It seemed to paralyze the city and lead to behavior you would never expect in normal times.

M. King Hubbert, by then age seventy, gloated to a rapidly convened energy course at Stanford that he had predicted this crisis in 1956. However, he said, though the crisis in 1973 seemed hard; the real test would be in the early part of the twenty-first century when global oil would peak. This would be, he believed, the biggest challenge that our oil-based civilization had ever faced. The glue would begin to come unstuck. Climate change was something that we were all beginning to understand, but its impacts seemed a long way off. Together they challenged us to see that reducing fossil fuels was the agenda we must face up to sooner or later—especially in our cities.

I have spent the past thirty years trying to create awareness on this issue and to help prepare our cities and rural regions for the new constraint. When the *ABC Catalyst* show dramatized the peak oil issue in 2005 it was the first time I had seen such a media story in Australia apart from a few newspaper articles in Perth (many of my colleagues in other Australian cities say they have never been able to publish in Sydney or

Melbourne papers if they used the words "peak oil"). In response to the show I received a number of e-mails, including one from a man who said that he was amazed that as an educated person he had never been exposed to this issue. He assumed it was an exaggeration so he followed it through on the Web and found a plethora of material that convinced him we were correct.

I have been in and out of politics as an elected councilor and advisor to politicians for the past thirty years. Resilience for politicians is about getting re-elected; for me it was about ensuring that cities like my own had a chance at a better future by being prepared for these long-term underlying issues like peak oil and climate change. But I tried to see how both kinds of resilience could be achieved and indeed could be merged.

My main achievements have been in getting electric rail systems built as they represented to me not only a better way to make a city work without oil but a market-oriented way to restructure the city in its land use patterns to be less car dependent. Most of all these rail systems seemed to generate a sense of hope in a city. The politicians loved it and won elections on the rail decisions.

I also learned that whenever politicians made decisions based on fear they ended up regretting it. Polls and the political advice might have suggested a certain policy direction to satisfy the fearmongers, but deep down they knew it wouldn't last and wasn't right. So I came to see that the resilience of cities was built on hope not fear and that we would cope with peak oil and climate change depending on whether the politics of hope or fear dominated in our cities. This book summarizes that journey.

How did I get into this too . . . ?
Tim Beatley

The oil crisis of the early 1970s had a personal and profound impact on me as a newly licensed teenage driver. Growing up in an excessively car-dependent American society, that driver's license translated into long-anticipated freedom and independence. The sudden (and incomprehensible to my young mind) appearance of hours-long (and miles-long) lines at the gas pumps virtually ended my car-mobility before it started. For at least a while I rediscovered my feet and the ability to function quite well without a car. But the notion that there might actually be finite limits to something that I assumed was limitless was a profound revelation, and the lines at the pump, and the chaos and anxiety that ensued, remain vivid memories of my youth.

These events have certainly helped to shape my own sense of need to be less reliant on oil, less dependent on any single resource, especially one with such serious environmental and social costs.

Many years later the opportunity of living in the Netherlands reawakened me to the virtues and possibilities of a life without a car, to the enriching possibilities of a life based on walking, bicycling, and public transit. Much of my professional and academic career has been spent focused on finding creative ways to plan and design highly livable urban environments, less car- (and oil-) dependent; places that at once strengthen our human connections and connectedness, and our bonds to the natural systems and landscapes that ultimately sustain us. Often we have gotten it wrong, of course, and my work on coastal policy and environmental planning has shown the dangers of a hubris and carelessness in how we treat natural systems, and a failure to understand the profound interconnectedness of urban and natural systems (can we continue to fill coastal wetlands, modify natural river systems, and ultimately alter planetary climate itself without severe impacts in cities like New Orleans?). I have also had the great fortune of studying and analyzing cities that are beginning to get it right, cities like London and New York and Stockholm, that are finally recognizing the practical and moral necessity of confronting climate change, taking steps to wean themselves off fossil fuels, and in the process forging hopeful, indeed exciting, urban futures.

For more than twenty years I have had the privilege of teaching a form of urban planning that blends an appreciation of local places with a sense of global responsibility. Peak oil and climate change present the field of planning an unprecedented opportunity to (help to) shape a more sustainable, healthy, and just urban future. These are challenging times for planners, to be sure, but the chance to make a difference has never been greater.

And me . . . ?
Heather Boyer

The themes running through this book are fear and hope, and these are ever present in the books I edit that earnestly detail the dangers of continuing with our current patterns of development, then provide plans, best practices, and examples of how we can create more livable, sustainable, resilient communities. On my journey I experienced many different types of urban living in Green Bay, Wisconsin; Minneapolis–St. Paul, Minnesota; Washington, D.C.; Boulder, Colorado; Cambridge, Massachusetts; and Brooklyn, New York. The city seen as the most sustainable—Boulder, is in fact a lovely, green oasis. But once leaving the inner-greenbelt bike paths (which are, gloriously, plowed immediately after a snow), getting around most places required a car (or a bus that was likely to be sitting in the same traffic). But there is much to be hopeful for in Colorado, with their new transit system (with planned TODs) for the Denver region.

From there I went to Cambridge to study design and development as a Loeb Fellow for one year. While it was an unbelievable opportunity (not to mention exciting to be back in a place with a rail system), I couldn't help but be disappointed in the lack of integration, or even mention, of sustainability issues in the design, real estate development, and affordable housing courses. What were the next generation of designers and developers learning? I see this changing not only in the curriculum at most design schools but in initiatives such as Architecture 2030 and the University and College Presidents Climate Change agreement. Not only are schools and universities changing how they teach about design, they are also teaching by showing how to retrofit their campus infrastructure to minimize their environmental impact.

I have been fearful about the future of our cities and the natural areas surrounding them, but hopeful at the recent recognition of climate change and initiatives to green urban areas. But these cities cannot be green unless they are inviting places to walk, bike, ride transit, and socialize. I fear that the real changes necessary to make cities sustainable and resilient, such as providing significantly greater support for transit, won't happen quickly enough. But I am hopeful to see that the change is beginning. I see the biking and pedestrian infrastructure changing in my own city of New York (in spite of the challenges of implementing congestion pricing). I see the success of the light rail in Minneapolis. I see what is now the most heavily used rails-to-trails project in Wisconsin built in my hometown. While I have little recollection of an administration in the White House trying to implement a federal urban policy, I remain hopeful that that will soon change too.

Acknowledgments

This book has had a long gestation. As described in the preface, Tim and Peter began to note an emerging serious issue with cities and their oil dependency in the 1970s. We were not alone in that concern and have had a lot of help in putting our fears and hopes on paper.

Families have been especially important to all of us as our lives in cities are primarily lived out through our families. Each of us owes a debt to our parents, partners, and children, who have been there to help us as we tried to reduce our footprints while improving our urban lifestyle opportunities. In particular we would like to thank Jan, Sam, Anneke, Carolena, Jadie, Doug, Barb, and Bob (who set an example by riding his bike year round in Wisconsin).

Communities give context to our work. Fremantle, Charlottesville, Boulder, and New York have each provided opportunities for us to practice our policies and learn how hard it is to generate hope for a more resilient city. There are many other cities that we have visited to draw inspiration for our book.

Institutions have enabled us to pursue our ideas. Our universities of Murdoch, Curtin, Virginia, and Harvard have given us the priceless opportunity to research and to teach about resilient cities. The Australian-American Fulbright Commission provided a Senior Scholarship to Peter to focus the book and the School of Architecture at the University of Virginia provided the Harry W. Porter Visiting Professorship, which enabled us to complete the book.

Particular thanks to colleagues who have contributed at various times should include Jeff Kenworthy, Anthony Perl, Randy Salzman, and Jeanne Liedtka.

1

Urban Resilience: Cities of Fear and Hope

Look at the world around you. It may seem like an immovable, implacable place.

It is not. With the slightest push—in just the right place—it can be tipped.

—Malcolm Gladwell, *The Tipping Point*

Resilience in our personal lives is about lasting, about making it through crises, about inner strength and strong physical constitution. Resilience is destroyed by fear, which causes us to panic, reduces our inner resolve, and eventually debilitates our bodies. Resilience is built on hope, which gives us confidence and strength. Hope is not blind to the possibility of everything getting worse, but it is a choice we make when faced with challenges. Hope brings health to our souls and bodies.

Resilience can be applied to cities. They too need to last, to respond to crises and adapt in a way that may cause them to change and grow differently; cities require an inner strength, a resolve, as well as a strong physical infrastructure and built environment.

Fear undermines the resilience of cities. The near or total collapse of many cities has been rooted in fear: health threats like the plague or yellow fever have struck cities and emptied them of those with the resources to escape, leaving only the poor behind. Invading armies have destroyed cities by sowing fear before an arrow or shot was fired. The racial fears of a generation in American cities decanted millions to the suburbs and beyond. Perhaps the biggest fear today in many cities is terrorism. In New York after 9/11, fear stopped people from congregating on streets or using the subway and sent many urban dwellers scurrying for the suburbs, but the city proved to be resilient and resisted collapse. After the terrorist bombings in London, the city immediately steeled itself to be normal, to resolve to go to work and to use the subway; signs appeared everywhere: "7 million Londoners, 1 London."

A danger that few think about with such immediacy is the threat of the collapse of our metropolitan regions in the face of resource depletion—namely, the reduction in the availability of oil and the necessary reduction in all fossil fuel use to reduce human impact on climate change. This book is not about introducing a new fear, but of understanding the implications of our actions and finding hope in the steps that can be taken to create resilient cities in the face of peak oil and climate change. Some cities exude hope as they grow and confront the future, others reek of fear as the processes of decline set in and the pain of change causes distrust and despair. Most cities have a combination of the two. For example, Atlanta is a city with some of the nation's worst traffic congestion (sixty hours of delay annually per traveler in 2005) and rapidly growing urban sprawl. While it is experiencing areas of abandonment as a result of the subprime mortgage meltdown, its inner city continues to grow, reclaiming old areas once abandoned and reversing the decline of generations.[1]

Atlanta has been dubbed a little Los Angeles for its similar sprawling highways and automobile dependence, but Los Angeles was ranked second lowest in carbon emissions (from transportation and residential buildings) per capita, while Atlanta ranks sixty-seventh.[2] However, cities of hope will use considerably less fuel and produce much less carbon than both of these in an age of carbon constraint.

Cities of fear make decisions based on short-term, even panicked, responses; cities of hope plan for the long term, with each decision building toward that vision, hopeful that some of the steps will be tipping points that lead to fundamental change. Cities of fear engage in competition as their only driving force, while cities of hope build consensus around cooperation and partnership. Cities of fear see threats everywhere while cities of hope see opportunities to improve in every crisis.

This book focuses on the challenges our metropolitan areas face in responding to their increasing carbon footprint, dependence on fossil fuels, and impact on our irreplaceable natural resources. Jared Diamond's book Collapse looks at how some settlements and regions have collapsed due to the inability to adapt, leading to an undermining of the natural resource base on which they depended. A characteristic of those societies appears to be that they became fixated by their fear of the future

Traffic in Los Angeles. In spite of its history of auto dependence, Los Angeles was ranked second in a 2008 study conducted by the Brookings Institution of the U.S. cities with the lowest carbon emissions. However, on this issue Los Angeles needs to be viewed in comparison to global cities (see Brown, Southworth, and Sarzynski report at www.brookings.edu). (Credit: iStockphoto.com)

and were unable to adapt. On the other hand, Diamond outlines examples of societies facing the same pressures that were able to adapt—they turned their hope into urban resilience.[3]

Diamond speculates on how climate change and resource degradation are threatening our cities and regions today. These are slow-moving phenomena that can undermine the continued growth of cities. Our book takes this potential of urban collapse seriously but is focused on how we *can* adapt to our present crises, how we *can* make our cities more resilient to the future in ways that are socially and economically acceptable and feasible.

The book takes the dual issues of peak oil and climate change as the key focus and rationale for our need to change. It describes how the production peak in global oil may already have occurred, or is very close at hand due to a combination of physical shortages and political control in vulnerable regions. For all practical purposes we must adapt our cities to lessen our dependence on petroleum. This is no small task as oil use in every city in the world has grown each year for most of the twentieth century; yet turning this trend around is within our reach. Global governance is recognizing the implications of climate change and the impact of cities, and there is a movement to require all cities to use less and less fossil fuel each year. This is no longer a speculative plea to cities, but is becoming a political and legal necessity.

Few would suggest that creating resilient cities is possible with technological advances alone, and agree that it must involve change in our cultures, our economies, and our lifestyles. It is the human capacity of our cities that is ultimately being tested by these challenges.

While understanding the implications of our current lifestyle is important, the response should not be driven by fear of collapse, but by the hopeful vision of the livable, equitable, resilient places our cities can become. We want to show that there is hope in our cities.

Why Concentrate on Cities?

Cities have grown rapidly in the age of cheap oil and now consume 75 percent of the world's energy and emit 80 percent of the world's greenhouse gases.[4] Cities are presently growing globally at 2 percent per year (over 3 percent in less developed regions and 0.7 percent in more developed regions), while rural areas have leveled out and are in many places declining. For the first time, half of humanity lives in cities, and it is estimated that by 2030 the number of city dwellers will reach five billion, or 60 percent, of the world's population.[5]

Urbanization has been happening since the Neolithic revolution when agriculture enabled food surpluses to create a division of labor in settlements. The unlocking of human ingenuity to work on technology, trade, and urban culture has created ever-expanding opportunities in cities. However, while some cities took advantage of these new opportunities, many remained as little more than rural trading posts. Urban opportunities accelerated with the Industrial Revolution and more recently with the globalization of the economy. But again not every city has taken advantage of these opportunities. Some cities, such as Liverpool, Philadelphia, and Pittsburgh, have struggled to adapt to the new opportunities and have relied for too long on outmoded methods of industrial production as the basis for their cities. Yet other cities, such as Manchester and New York, have made the transition and are thriving.

Peter Hall, who has examined why some cities adapt more rapidly than others, suggests that the desire to experiment and innovate is found in the heart of the city's culture. Robert Friedel calls it the "culture of improvement," Lewis Mumford refers to this instinct in a city as a "collective work of art," and Tim Gorringe as "creative spirituality."[6] Whatever it is called, the ability to experiment and innovate is the tissue of hope and the core of resilience.

Overcoming the fear of change today must involve new experiments in green urbanism, as cities seek to improve themselves in ways that fit their culture. Which cities will respond to the new set of opportunities opening up around this global sustainability issue? Rethinking how we create our built environment is critical in lessening our dependence on oil and minimizing our carbon footprint. Buildings produce 43 percent of the world's carbon dioxide emissions and consume 48 percent of the energy produced. It is projected that by shifting 60 percent of new growth to compact patterns the United States will save 85 million metric tons of carbon dioxide annually by 2030.[7] We believe that the change, when dealing with global issues like peak oil and climate change, needs to come from cities. Nations can do a lot to help or hinder these efforts, but the really important initiatives have to begin at the city level because there is great variation in how cities cope with issues within any nation. Great leadership and innovation can be found in cities. For example, while the United States has yet to ratify the Kyoto Protocol, over 825 mayors of U.S. cities signed onto the U.S. Mayors Climate Protection Agreement to commit their city to reaching the goals of the Protocol. The initiative, which was spearheaded by Seattle Mayor Greg Nickels, strives to meet these goals through leadership and action advanced by a network of forward-thinking cities large and small. Similarly the Clinton Foundation has coordinated an approach to reducing greenhouse gases for the big cities in the world through its C40 Large Cities Climate Leadership Group, an association of large global cities dedicated to tackling climate change.[8]

Our book tells many of these stories of hope in cities across the globe, which show there is leadership coming from government, industry, universities, and community groups. Although its focus is on American cities where so much more is needed, many of the examples will come from elsewhere in the world.

What Are Resilient Cities?

Since the devastation of many Gulf Coast cities from Hurricane Katrina in 2005, the Indian Ocean tsunami of 2004 that impacted eleven countries, and the Burmese cyclone of 2008, resilient cities have most often been discussed in relation to the city's ability to respond to a natural disaster. Here we use an expanded definition to include a city's ability to respond to a natural resource shortage and respond to the recognition of the human impact on climate change. There is debate about the link between climate change and natural disasters, which has been renewed as scientists try to understand the increasing incidence of devastating natural disasters, such as the super cyclones that devastated New Orleans and Myanmar.[9]

We have focused on the idea of resilient cities as those that can substantially reduce their dependence on petroleum fuels in ways that are socially and economically acceptable and feasible. But whether the impetus for pursuing resiliency is to respond to natural or to human made disasters, the outcome is similar. Resilient cities have built-in systems that can adapt to change, such as a diversity of transport and land-use systems and multiple sources of renewable power that will allow a city to survive shortages in fuel supplies.[10]

Brian Walker, David Salt, and Walter Reid have summarized the academic area of "resilience thinking," which has emerged as a way of managing ecosystems like coral reefs or farming systems and other complex social-economic-ecological systems. Their principles of resilience are applicable to cities. They write, "Resilience is the capacity of a system to absorb disturbance and still retain its basic function and structure." Tabatha Wallington, Richard Hobbes, and Sue Moore say that ecological resilience "may be measured by the magnitude of disturbance the system can tolerate and still persist." This book attempts to apply this concept to the complex social-economic-ecological systems of cities.[11]

In New Orleans the resilience of the city to withstand winds and waves from Katrina was reduced by the loss of wetlands and mangroves around the Gulf shores, and by the inadequate infrastructure provided by the levees. But the main human disaster came about because the transit system was so inadequate that people who did not own a car (around a third of the population) could not evacuate, and the freeways were at capacity due to the number of individuals in cars. No plan for using school buses and other transit vehicles was in place, so those resources were all washed away with the first floods. The transport system was not resilient and it undermined the rest of the urban system, which turned rapidly into social chaos.

In a resilient city every step of development and redevelopment of the city will make it more sustainable: it will reduce its ecological footprint (consumption of land, water, materials, and energy, especially the oil so critical to their economies, and the output of waste and emissions) while simultaneously improving its quality of life (environment, health, housing, employment, community) so that it can better fit within the capacities of local, regional, and global ecosystems. Resilience needs to be applied to all the natural resources on which cities rely.[12]

In resilience thinking the more sustainable a city the more it will be able to cope with reductions in the resources that are used to make the city work. Sustainability recognizes there are limits in the local, regional, and global systems within which cities fit, and that when those limits are breached the city can rapidly decline. The more a city can minimize its dependence on resources such as fossil fuels in a period when there are global constraints on supply and global demand is increasing, the more resilient it will be. Atlanta needs 782 gallons of gasoline per person each year for its urban system to work, but in Barcelona it is just 64 gallons. With oil supply cuts and carbon taxes the decline in availability of oil will seriously confront Atlanta, yet Barcelona is likely to cope with ease. Both cities will still need to have plans in place that help their citizenry cope with such a disturbance.[13]

Why Should Cities Move Toward Resiliency?

Resiliency in cities can be rationalized by simply understanding why we need to reduce oil dependence in urban regions.

- *Reducing oil use is a political necessity.* The waning of petroleum resources and the global climate change imperatives discussed in this book require all cities to act; if they don't their citizenry will suffer from the inevitable increase in prices, as we are seeing in the U.S. right now. The $100-a-barrel oil barrier has been broken and some analysts are saying that it could go over $300 within five years.[14]
- *Reducing oil use will reduce impacts on the environment.* Oil use is responsible for approximately one-third of greenhouse gases.

New Orleans was one of the first modern cities to be destroyed by a climate change–induced phenomenon. Its resilience will require rebuilding natural and human infrastructure as well as plans that include the carless poor. [Credit: iStockphoto.com (top); Timothy Beatley (bottom)]

Transport greenhouse is seen as the most worrying part of the climate change agenda as it continues to grow during a period when more renewable or efficient options are available.

- *Reducing oil use and investing in green buildings will reduce impacts on human health.* Improvements in urban air quality from

Rebuilding a community—the Habitat for Humanity Musicians' Village.
(see www.resilientcitiesbook.org) (Credit: Peter Newman)

technological advances are being washed out by growing use of vehicles. Thirty-nine different air quality districts are over the required standards (this is 40 percent of the United States). Developing cities desperately need to lower air emissions as they are often well above WHO recommended health limits.[15] Other health issues, such as obesity due to lack of activity, as well as stress and depression could be reduced by minimizing auto dependence.

In the United States buildings account for 36 percent of energy use and 30 percent of greenhouse gas emissions. The immediate benefits of natural sunlight, however, go beyond energy savings and reducing our impact on climate change. Studies show that people in proximity to natural daylight are more productive and healthier. Workers in green buildings report fewer sick days and are more productive. When schools have gone green, test scores have improved.[16] Green buildings are attracting developers now not just because they can reduce their ongoing costs but because their tenants and purchasers want a more healthy and productive building in which to live, learn, and work. The urban heat island effect from the waste heat generated has also been problematic. For example, this has been a motivation for Mayor Daley in

Chicago to green his city after an extreme summer heat wave proved to be fatal.

- *Reducing oil use will result in greater equity and economic gain.* The inequities of heavily car dependent cities for the elderly, the young, and the poor, will be reduced by greater walkability and transit access; the social issues such as noise, neighborhood severance, road rage, and loss of public safety will be reduced; the economic costs from loss of productive agricultural land to sprawl and bitumen, the costs of accidents, pollution, and congestion, all will be reduced.[17]

- *Reducing our dependence on petroleum fuels will make us less economically vulnerable.* The next agenda for the global economy, sometimes called the Sixth Wave (see chapter 2), is about responding with technology and services for a new and more clever kind of resource use. Cities will compete within this economic framework, and those cities that get in first will likely do best. But the same economic competition is facing households, depending on which city they live in and where they live in those cities. In U.S. cities the proportion of household expenditure on transportation increased from 10 percent in the 1960s to 19 percent in 2005, before the 2006 oil price increases (which only reduced the percentage to 18 percent), with very car dependent cities like Houston and Detroit having even higher percentages. A more detailed study by the Center for Housing Policy shows working families with household incomes between $20,000 and $50,000 spend almost 30 percent of their income on transportation. In Atlanta within this income range the percentage is 32 and for families who have found cheap housing on the fringe, transportation can account for over 40 percent of their expenses. In Australia surveys show that 40 percent of household income goes to transportation in some urban fringe areas. Almost all of this is for car travel. Households on the fringes of car-dependent cities are more vulnerable as the cost of transport escalates, especially after oil reached one hundred dollars a barrel in late 2007 (at one hundred and thirty-nine dollars a barrel as we go to press). This increase in oil prices coincided with the subprime mortgage crisis, hitting many with a double whammy of increased transportation costs and a ballooning mortgage payment. Cities, and parts of cities, are now economically vulnerable to oil as it increases in cost.[18]

- *Reducing dependence on foreign oil is likely to result in more resilient, peaceful cities.* Cities that are able to successfully reduce their dependence on imported oil, especially from politically sensitive areas, will have greater energy security. Terrorism and war have many causes, but one deep and underlying issue is the need by high-oil-consuming countries to secure access to oil in foreign areas, whether they are friendly or not. As oil becomes more and more valuable, the security of supply will become a more and more central part of geopolitics. Fear can drive us to make security decisions that are not going to help create resilient cities. Thus underneath all these arguments is the fact that reducing our oil dependence—*could result in less war.*

Most importantly we are convinced that resilient cities will be better places to live. The many benefits of a resilient city include greater overall physical and emotional health; ease of movement in higher density, mixed-use communities that are walkable and have accessible transit options; better food that is produced locally and is therefore fresher; efficiency of energy resources, greater affordability, healthier indoor environments; easier access to natural environments; and more awareness of the local urban area and its bioregion enabling us to have a greater sense of place and identity. Some of these factors are challenging to quantify-but are nevertheless real opportunities that will emerge from this book.[19]

No models are readily available to illustrate this positive approach to cities in the age of reduced oil availability. Most cities have strategic plans based on coping with anticipated growth in population, and a growing number of cities have sustainability plans to handle this growth in an environmentally sound manner. All Australian cities, for example, have recently had strategic planning studies done for the next thirty years of development. Although the studies have recognized that there is a need to reduce automobile dependence and save on oil, the government has not intervened in any radical way to curb oil-consuming behavior, even with the recognition that urbanization is likely to continue and tax already strained resources. New York City is a similar example. On Earth Day 2007 Mayor Bloomberg released an ambitious twenty-five-year plan for a greener city, which goes as far as committing to a 30 percent reduction in greenhouse gases by 2030. But it is not clear how the city plans to achieve this reduction, though there is pressure from urban design groups to require developers to analyze and disclose their impacts on

New York is demonstrating its resilience after the 9/11 attacks. The Freedom Tower at the Ground Zero site (scheduled to be completed in 2009) will be a green building featuring an urban wind farm and solar panels. (Courtesy of Skidmore, Owings & Merrill LLP)

climate change before having their projects approved (79 percent of New York City's greenhouse gas emissions are produced by buildings).[20]

Few cities anywhere have focused on the transportation implications of reducing their oil dependence. San Francisco passed a resolution recognizing peak oil in April 2006 and fourteen other U.S. cities have followed suit, but none of these cities have a detailed plan for reducing their oil use. Austin, Texas, approved a Climate Protection Plan in 2008, which has many innovative features but almost no reference to transportation. Many cities do have plans for reducing their dependence on oil for energy use. For example, the city of Hamilton in Ontario, Canada, has developed an energy strategy, which includes the promotion of clean, renewable electricity such as wind, solar, and water power, but energy rarely is taken to mean gasoline.[21]

Cities of course cannot be separated from their hinterlands or bioregions. Although rural regions have generally been declining or are at least static (apart from the movement of people to the coasts in wealthy countries), they also have increased in their oil dependence. Rural economic productivity based on agriculture, tourism, and mining has been growing based on cheap oil. These activities have a large component of oil for travel in the case of tourism, and both agriculture and mining use diesel for transport, machinery, and processing, and also depend on chemicals (especially fertilizer in agriculture's case) made from oil. Food is now transported huge distances, with an average U.S. meal taking between 1,300 and 2,000 "food miles" to reach the plate.[22]

While the focus of this book is on cities, it will also look at questions facing rural regions around cities as they relate to resiliency. What will happen to this rural productivity in the age of declining oil availability? How will cities and their associated rural regions cope? Where do you start in responding to this issue?

While environmentalists are quite able to point out the limitations of current resource consumption trends, they are often criticized for their inability to set forth a positive and compelling alternative vision. Michael Shellenberger and Ted Norhaus have called this the "death of environmentalism." There is a certain amount of truth to this claim as it is always easier to criticize than to suggest the next step. And when it comes to these global issues it can become hard to focus constructively. But this book will show us how we can respond to these twin crises.[23]

What Do Resilient Cities Look Like?

What could happen to the world's cities if we ignore the need to reduce oil? What will our cities actually look like if we do seriously reduce our dependence on oil? Not much can be projected from recent experience as it is described as a point of "singularity" (a term from science fiction about what is beyond black holes). Trends cannot just be extended to see the future when we are dealing with discontinuities. Nor can we just turn history back to cities as they were. Few people could see what industrialization would do to cities; few could anticipate the global knowledge economy and what cheap oil would do to cities. But there are lessons to be learned from history and the fate of cities that have not been able or willing to adapt. So we have looked at some of the speculation about collapse and how some cities are adapting and others are not adapting. We are more interested in what we can do to *change* our cities so they start to become more resilient.

According to urban critic Jane Jacobs, cities throughout history have competed by examining innovations in other cities and building upon them. This, she believes, is the basis of wealth creation. We see the response to climate change and peak oil as the impetus for the next burst of innovation. This book looks at those innovative cities that are beginning to grasp this new agenda and have moved (often timidly) down the track toward change. There are only a few cities around the world showing such leadership, as most are watching tentatively. It is our belief that those cities that begin this transition first will manage better socially and economically in a world where the constraints on petroleum fuels will be pressing.[24]

Although no one can predict the future of cities, we are able to visualize where we use gasoline, diesel, heating oil, and natural gas, and then try to imagine home, neighborhood, and region without them. How might they look and feel if these resources were not available, or at least were in decline, so that each next step in development or redevelopment had to show how it would help to wean us off these resources? Can we imagine a city where we radically reduce the amount of driving we do? This is not simply a set of abstract arguments about the fate of the planet, but something that has relevance and is potentially understandable to everyone in terms of the places in which we all live. A future can then be imagined that involves alternative energy sources as well as funding for the design of transit and bicycling systems and the creation or redevelopment of buildings, communities, cities, and regions around the need for less petroleum fuel.

Conclusion

This book is about resilient cities and how they can be designed to provide a practical and realistic set of options for responding to our current oil dependency and overconsumption of all fossil fuel resources. Fear paralyzes us when we can't see a viable next step. We want to inspire and enable urban dwellers, planners, designers, and policymakers to learn from innovations and stories in other cities to see that there is not only know-how, but momentum and hope for creating more resilient cities.

2

Climate Change and Peak Oil: The Double Whammy for Resource-Intensive Cities

In June 2008 the price of oil reached one hundred and forty dollars a barrel and the impacts, both positive and negative, were evident across the globe. According to *USA Today*, "Americans drove 30 billion fewer miles from November through April than during the same period in 2006–07, the biggest such drop since the Iranian revolution led to gasoline supply shortages in 1979–80."[1] In Portugal fishermen were protesting as they could no longer afford the diesel for their fishing boats; in England a convoy of trucks blocked roads into London as they protested high fuel prices; the aviation industry began to spiral down; in cities around the developing world people were rioting over food prices that were in part bloated by the fuel crisis. Whole suburban streets were being boarded up and abandoned in some fringe areas of U.S. cities. Motor vehicle manufacturers again reassured us they could produce more fuel efficient cars. Politicians were either blaming banks for artificially inflating the oil price through speculation or OPEC for artificially keeping the supply down, and financial analysts were pointing a finger at the high taxes on fuel. Will we learn from this fuel shortage?

During the 1973–1974 OPEC oil embargo, U.S. cities began to unravel as drivers joined gas queues for four or five hours to fill their tanks, fuel was being removed at gun point, and many people were paralyzed with fear and simply stayed at home.[2]

At no other stage in the history of the U.S. car culture has there been a physical oil shortage to test the resiliency of cities as there was during the oil embargo. Yet the actual reduction in oil flowing to the United States due to the OPEC embargo was just 4 percent as other sources were available and the U.S. produced almost 80 percent of its own needs.

This chapter looks at the current test facing cities—the combination of peak oil and climate change. There will need to be further reductions in demand for petroleum and all other fossil fuels that will inevitably have to be introduced by government policy. The resilience of heavily car-dependent and petroleum-dependent cities will be severely tested.

Climate Change

The momentum of global agreement on the need to address climate change has been inexorable and accelerating. In November 2007, United Nations Secretary General Ban Ki-moon described climate change as "the defining challenge of our age."[3]

Al Gore's 2006 movie, *An Inconvenient Truth*, was enormously effective in relaying an easily digestible message to the general public about the dangers of global warming. Gore continues to work with organizations, policymakers, and citizens to help them understand the implications of climate change and what can be done to minimize our impact.[4]

In 2006 the U.K. government's treasury head Sir Nicholas Stern showed the financial world the potential costs of inaction, stating that climate change "is the greatest and widest-ranging market failure ever seen." The report estimates many possible economic implications of climate change, including the cost of extreme weather events. "Heat waves like that experienced in 2003 in Europe, when 35,000 people died and agricultural losses reached $15 billion, will be commonplace by the middle of the century."[5]

The world's climate scientists have been meeting under the United Nations Intergovernmental Panel on Climate Change (IPCC) for twenty years. Their 2007 report said that global warming is "unequivocal" and that human activity is "very likely" to be the cause of the rise in temperatures since 1950. While this is the fourth report released by the panel since 1990, it is the first report in which they have stated without question that global warming is a fact, and that human impact is a significant cause (with 90 percent certainty). Al Gore and the IPCC shared the Nobel Peace Prize in 2007 "for their efforts to build up and disseminate greater knowledge about man-made climate change, and to lay the foundations for the measures that are needed to counteract such change."[6]

When popular culture, finance and science are saying the same thing, the political momentum is unstoppable. And thus even the climate-skeptic nations of the United States and Australia joined the global process to accept the need for change.

The U.S. congressional elections in 2006 reflected the new politics when the Democratic majority was formed and the first attempts at climate change–related bills followed, often with bipartisan support. No longer was it a question of whether you believed in climate change or not but who had the best policy on clean energy. Al Gore described the Australian federal election of 2007 as the first ever to be held in which climate change was the main topic. The resulting avalanche for Kevin Rudd over John Howard (who had a death-bed conversion to being a climate supporter but was not taken seriously after a decade of skepticism) led directly to the new cabinet signing Kyoto as their first act of government on December 3, 2007. That week at the UN Climate Conference in Bali, Australia was given a standing ovation. But perhaps of more significance at the end of the conference, when almost all hope had been lost for a global agreement, the United States decided to join the next stage of global governance on climate change (despite not ratifying Kyoto) in which the world will develop a plan by the end of 2009 for real reductions in fossil fuels through a global carbon phase-out commitment.

For those who continue to feel that this global governance will not lead anywhere, it is worth remembering how effective the process was of phasing out chlorofluorocarbons (CFCs), which scientists concluded in 1984 were a catalytic agent in ozone destruction. The potential for devastating environmental and human health outcomes spurred the world's climate scientists to begin a global awareness process immediately, which led to the Montreal Protocol on Substances that Deplete the Ozone Layer in 1987. The international treaty called for phasing out the production of substances that are harmful to the ozone layer. In subsequent UN conferences the requirements were reexamined and tightened. We learned to adapt in our cities, mostly through scientific research and technological advances, and the ozone hole is now recovering.[7]

Global governance worked because of partnerships between industry, community, and governments across the globe. It should be a great source of hope to us. But we should keep in mind that peak oil and climate change require much more significant changes in how we live, and are a bigger test of our faith in human civilization and our ability to make cities work.

Now we face the astonishing fact that we have altered the whole atmosphere to such an extent that we are losing Arctic ice at a rate of double the size of France every two years. Antarctic ice is accelerating in its decline by 70 percent over ten years. Increased storms and rising sea levels threaten cities everywhere, and New Orleans remains as a specter of what can happen.[8]

Cities and Climate Change

Although city dwellers emit less carbon on a per capita basis, the rapid urbanization of the globe means cities are emitting more carbon as a whole—accounting for close to 80 percent of all carbon dioxide, and contributing significantly to other greenhouse gases.[9] They also provide the greatest opportunity to lessen emissions due to the high-density development, walkability, and availability of or potential for mass transit.

The activities that produce the greatest contribution to global warming are concentrated in urban areas—transport, industry, buildings (in the U.S.: industry, 30 percent; transportation, 28 percent; commercial, 17 percent; residential, 17 percent; and agriculture, 8 percent).

Studies show that higher-density development results in lower greenhouse gas emissions from transport. Most programs to reduce emissions in transportation focus on vehicle fuel efficiency; however, studies show that our increased dependence on the automobile will wipe out any gains from vehicles that offer greater fuel efficiency. "The U.S. Department of Energy's Energy Information Administration (EIA) forecasts that driving will increase 59 percent between 2005 and 2030, outpacing the projected 23 percent increase in population. The EIA also forecasts a fleetwide fuel economy improvement of 12 percent within this time frame. Despite this improvement in efficiency, CO_2 emissions would grow by 41 percent."[10] This will not be allowed to occur if the international governance system is given any credence over climate change.

Global governance is now focused on how the world will prevent atmospheric average temperatures from increasing by more than 2 to 2.5 degrees Celsius. Beyond this there will be a loss of over one quarter of the world's biodiversity, and storms and hurricanes will become so intense that whole coastal areas will have to be abandoned, including many of the world's great cities.[11]

According to the IPCC, preventing this rise in temperature will require the world to reduce greenhouse gas emissions by at least 50 percent by 2050. The world's cities now must face the policy challenge of peaking consumption of fossil fuels followed by an inevitable, exponential decline, in part due to the peaking of supplies in oil and natural gas (referred to jointly as petroleum).

Peak Oil

"Peak oil" refers to the "maximum rate of the production of oil in any area under consideration, recognizing that it is a finite natural resource, subject to depletion."[12]

Oil producers know from years of experience that every oil field goes through a production cycle of increase–peak–decline. When oil fields in a region are aggregated geophysicists can model and predict when the area will peak and then decline. While new technology may extend their lifetimes, all oil fields eventually decline. Although half of the oil remains at the peak in production, the other half of the oil becomes harder to extract, as it increasingly fills with water and requires more energy to be pumped out. Eventually, as wells are abandoned, the region loses importance and drilling moves to other regions, often in increasingly more difficult and often sensitive areas (e.g., the Arctic National Wildlife Refuge or ANWAR).

National oil supplies can be examined to see how they appear in this cycle of oil depletion. After a nation peaks in its oil then a very different set of economic and political factors come into play as it must look elsewhere to meet growing oil demand. Indonesia and China have recently joined the group of oil-importing nations who were once exporters (over thirty countries have crossed this peak in the past thirty or so years).

The United States began to import oil after 1970 when its oil production peaked, which led to the strengthening of OPEC and the geopolitics of oil in the last part of the twentieth century. The United States now imports over half of its oil at a cost of $2.16 billion in mid-2008 (the Web site zfacts.com shows a continuous scrolling total of what oil imports are costing the U.S. In June 2008 it was nearly $4 trillion).

The idea of peak oil dates back to 1956 when a geophysicist for Shell Oil in Houston, Texas, Marion King Hubbert, suggested that oil production in any region would follow a bell-shaped curve with a peak followed by decline. The United States, he said, would peak in oil production in 1970. Despite being greeted with derision by many economists who believed that any supply issue would follow demand, the peak happened as predicted, and U.S. oil has continued to decline ever since despite a series of incentives and subsidies.

The same story is now happening to world oil. Global discoveries of new oil supplies have been on the decline since the 1960s, as shown in figure 2.1.

Global oil production generally has followed the bell-shaped Hubbert curve (apart from reductions due to the three oil crises of 1973, 1979, and 1991), and was on an upward trend until 2005. Since 2006 oil production has plateaued despite there being increased demand of around 2 to 3 percent (mainly due to China and India, though together they still only take 12 percent of world oil production while the U.S. takes 26 percent).

Understandably, the oil and car companies have been reluctant to admit to a peak in oil production due to the potential impact on their share price. But some have broken ranks to address the reality of peak oil, including the CEO of General Motors, who mentioned it at the Detroit Motor Show in 2008.[12] The CEO of Royal Dutch Shell on January 30, 2007, was the first of the oil majors to admit that there was now "an end to easy oil" and predicted a "worldwide scramble," especially after 2015.[13]

The *Wall Street Journal* front page article in November 2007 "Oil Officials See Limit Looming on Production," said that practical politics means that there is likely to be no more than 100 million barrels a day produced from the world's oil wells and perhaps less. This is due to the high depletion rates of many peaking wells, which have been over-pumped to keep production expanding (slower pumping would lead to a slower decline) and to the political turmoil in the Middle East (where the biggest deposits remain), Nigeria, and Venezuela. While the article distanced itself from peak oil theory, it discussed the issue of practical availability, which is the theory's basis.[14]

The notion of peak oil continues to be debated in many circles. Cambridge Energy Research Associates (CERA), an oil industry consultancy, predicts that oil production could rise to 112 million barrels of oil per day in 2017 (compared to 91 million gallons per day in 2007). In a high-profile response to this forecast, the Association for the Study of Peak Oil and Gas (ASPO) bet CERA a hundred thousand dollars that production will not reach these levels by 2017. ASPO believes that the age of peak oil is near, which means that oil is getting more challenging to find and the era of cheap oil is over forever.[15]

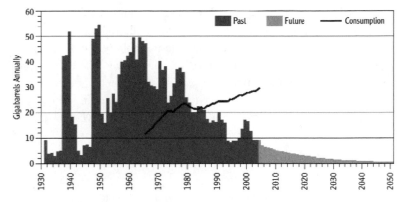

Figure 2.1. Global discoveries of new oil supplies have been on the decline since the 1960s. Global oil consumption, on the other hand, has risen substantially since then; a trajectory that cannot continue. (Adapted from work by Colin Campbell, ASPO)

In addition to CERA, other naysayers include Australian politician Bill Heffernan, who says peak oil will not happen for forty years, and Exxon, which claimed in 2007 that peak oil will not occur for at least twenty-five years.

Many governments have been reluctant to address the issue of peak oil; it is rarely in their interest to threaten something as fundamental as their constituents' oil dependence. But most of all, the community at large has seemed unwilling to think about the implications of increasing oil scarcity, and seems to be concerned only with the short-term implications on the price of oil. *The Guardian*, in an article called "Bottom of the Barrel—The World Is Running Out of Oil, So Why Do Politicians Refuse to Talk About It?" concluded:

> Every generation has its taboo, and ours is this: that the resource upon which our lives have been built is running out. We don't talk about it because we cannot imagine it. This is a civilization in denial.[16]

For the past few decades of debate on peak oil the International Energy Agency (IEA), a group created to advise twenty-seven member countries on energy policy, has been a peak oil skeptic. They have always said that enough oil resources remain to enable us to proceed for fifty years with business as usual. However, in 2006 the IEA recognized that *conventional oil is peaking* and may decline by as much as 5 percent. This is a remarkable admission. But they then suggest that, unlike all the other declining oil fields, the next batch of oil fields will be pushed much harder so that they will not decline in the traditional manner. They believe much more can be squeezed out of conventional wells to ease us through the next few years and allow time for alternatives to develop. Critics of this report raise considerable questions about the potential for "pushing" conventional oil. The level of alternatives that can be produced to fill the looming gap in oil supply received the biggest critique.[17]

Enormous effort has gone into trying to discover new oil reserves and to extract more from the reserves that remain. The discovery of new oil reserves is now growing at a much slower rate than oil is being consumed (at least one in three). According to Jim Buckee the CEO of the Canadian oil firm Talisman:

> Even with all the improved technology and continued exploration, we haven't reversed, or even really affected, the general downward trend from the global peak in oil discoveries that occurred in 1965. That suggests the problem is geological, rather than a human inability to find it. It's not there to be found."[18]

Most oil reserves are in the hands of OPEC, but analysts from the Association for the Study of Peak Oil and Gas are concerned about the reality of some Middle Eastern reserves (especially Saudi Arabia). In past decades some Middle Eastern suppliers have created "phantom reserves" to drive higher OPEC quotas on production. Quotas are given to countries on the basis of the size of their oil reserves. These quotas amount to licenses to make money in a world willing to pay for more oil.[19]

We believe that a peak in global oil production is inevitable. There are various estimates of when the peak will occur but they cluster around the early part of this century, with a few (now mostly discredited) projections far into the future. C. J. Campbell, an oil geophysicist who founded ASPO, says that conventional oil peaked in 2004 and all oil liquids will peak in 2010. Princeton University geologist Kenneth Deffeys believes that we have already reached peak production and we are now living in a "permanent state of shortage."[20]

An Australian television show on peak oil (*ABC Catalyst*, November 2005) reported the story of an Australian oil company CEO who had asked the attendees at the 2004 Australian Petroleum Production and Exploration Association whether they thought the global oil production peak had already occurred; half raised their hands.

More conservative estimates from government sources in the United Kingdom and the United States are saying that the oil peak will occur sometime between 2010 and 2020. Many commentators are now suggesting that "world oil is peaking" rather than precisely positioning a peak date, as production appears to have plateaued and is likely to remain level for some time. Half of the world's oil is coming from 15 percent of the world's reserves, which are being pumped to capacity. Some oil-producing regions are refusing to pump their reserves any harder so they can extend their lifetime. The "swing" producers like Saudi Arabia, which in the past always helped out the West by pushing out a bit more of their production, now are facing limits due to their production capacity, their rapidly growing internal consumption, and the start of the decline in some of their big wells. (In 2008 King Abdullah of Saudi Arabia declared that they should consider cutting back production for the sake of future generations.)

We seem to be on a plateau in terms of available oil, but how long can we push production before availability begins to dip and decline?[21]

We need to come up with short-term adaptations for our cities in the face of declining oil, while we plan for longer-term change. Time is needed to do the necessary research and testing on alternative fuel sources. Michael Pacheco of the National Renewable Energy Laboratory (NREL)'s National Bioenergy Center says that whatever the peak "We need to start working toward replacement fuels 20 years before that peak." So it is likely that we are already well behind schedule in responding adequately to this challenge.[22]

Acknowledging and responding to the problems related to our automobile dependency challenges every aspect of life. We have spent the past sixty plus years building our cities and rural regions around the availability of cheap oil and now must contemplate a different future. In 2007, globally, more than 70 million new cars and light trucks were built, which include a growing proportion of SUVs with 500 HP V8 engines consuming 25 to 30 liters of gasoline per 100 kilometers. Although with current record gas prices and a depressed economy, sales of large cars have slowed down in America, evidenced by the closure of car manufacturing plants and desperation deals such as free gas with the purchase of a car.

New challenges are anticipated by innovations such as the Tata People's car, the Nano, to be available in India for around 2,500 U.S. dollars. While it makes car ownership available to many who could not previously afford it, it is likely to lead to increased oil consumption, air pollution, and congestion.[23]

Can it go on?

Natural Gas: Savior or Same Problem?

Natural gas is a "combustible mix of hydrocarbon gases" primarily made up of methane, but can also include ethane, propane, butane, and pentane. While capturing methane requires drilling, natural gas is clean burning and is an obvious transition fuel to help ease the problem of oil depletion as it results in about two-thirds of the greenhouse gases compared to oil and three-fifths compared to coal. It can be converted to diesel as well as being used in vehicles in its original form. Natural gas has already been used to replace heating oil in many homes and to replace oil used in commerce and industry. In Australia oil went from 57 percent of the fuel mix in 1980–81 to 48 percent in 1997–98 while natural gas went from 13 percent to 20 percent as boilers, kilns, stoves, and heaters all shifted to natural gas.[24]

The next stage would thus appear to be to switch to greater use of natural gas in transport as trucks and trains and fishing boats can use CNG (compressed natural gas) or LNG (liquefied natural gas) in their diesel engines. Cars can be switched over as well (particularly if the manufacturer makes them standard as occurred in Sweden when the government committed to natural gas cars for their vehicle fleet). The attraction is that the infrastructure for capturing natural gas is already in place, although filling stations are not commonplace.

The conversion to natural gas is an obvious step in places like Australia where there is a good supply of natural gas available. However in Europe and in the United States this is not the case. Europe is going to faraway places to the east, such as Russia, to obtain their gas, and already some signs of an OPEC-like protection of the resource are developing. In the United States natural gas has already peaked and officials are now looking to import it using LNG tankers—starting an overseas dependence similar to that for oil.

Global natural gas production has had estimates on its peak similar to those for oil production, although with slightly less certainty; estimates range from 2010 to 2030. The peak in discoveries occurred in the late 1960s to early 1970s so the same pattern as oil seems to be evident. It is not surprising that oil and natural gas patterns are parallel as they have similar geological origins in marine sediment (unlike coal, which comes from ancient forests). In addition, oil and natural gas prices are closely linked so as oil goes up in price the same is likely to occur for natural gas. Natural gas can only be a small part of the transitional arrangement for oil; it cannot be seen as the long-term replacement as it is also peaking. Moreover its use will need to be phased out eventually as part of our response to climate change.[25] The benefit of the transition to natural gas is that it enables the long-term transition to hydrogen to be facilitated.

How Are Oil and Natural Gas Used?

Average individuals in the United States in 2006 (as it crossed the 300 million population mark) consumed 880 gallons of oil and natural gas products in their vehicles and buildings. This is 880 gallons that they cannot assume will be there in the next twenty to thirty years. Indeed as outlined below, the fuels in the 880 gallons used per person in the United States (gasoline 473 gallons, diesel 120 gallons, heating oil 90 gallons, natural gas in buildings equivalent to 197 gallons) will need to be at least halved by 2050.

Table 2.1 shows the proportion of U.S. oil that is used in its various components and table 2.2 does the same for natural gas.

Although the United States is the worst offender, we need to understand globally how fuels are used and how we can reduce our dependence on them. This is the physical reality that must define the agenda of the world's cities.

Are There Alternatives to Oil?

The response from many economists to the idea of peak oil is that supply and demand will create the necessary change, and thus alternatives to oil

Table 2.1   Uses of Oil

Gasoline—for automobiles	47%
Diesel—for trucks, boats, freight trains, and some cars, plus some power plants	13%
Jet fuel—for planes	10%
Heating oil—buildings	10%
LPG—taxis and fleets	4%
Asphalt—paving	3%
Petrochemicals—chemicals, plastics, rubber, clothing, pharmaceuticals, etc.	18%

Sources: EIA Web site, October 30, 2006, and EIA Annual Energy Outlook, 2006.

Table 2.2   Uses of Natural Gas

Use	Proportion (in U.S., 2003)
Industry—fertilizer, steel, glass, paper, clothing, bricks, etc.	37%
Residential—heating, cooking, water heating	23%
Electric power	23%
Commercial—heating buildings, etc.	14%
Transport	5%

Source: EIA, Annual Energy Review.

will seamlessly fill the gap (see box 2.1). Technological modernism and the idea of substitutability of resources due to price is still the most powerful paradigm of our age. "The Stone Age didn't end with a shortage of stones" is a statement frequently heard when oil depletion is debated (attributed to Sheik Yamani the founder of OPEC). However, there seems to be something quite different and challenging about oil as it is so fundamental to everything we do and is likely to involve a considerably more expensive set of alternatives that have not easily emerged. An additional challenge to alternative fuels is the fact that the process of extraction results in significant energy output and in most cases a significant output of greenhouse gas emissions. Alex Farrell, a professor in the Energy and Resources Group at the University of California–Berkeley suggests that "all unconventional forms of oil are worse for greenhouse-gas emissions than petroleum." For example, Canada, one of the first signatories of the Kyoto Protocol, is unlikely to reach the target it set for CO_2 reduction largely due to its extensive oil extraction operation in the Alberta Tar Sands.[26] A report by the Canadian environmental group Environmental Defence claims that "Canada's progress on global warming is being held hostage by the tar sands," and that the tar sands are "ground zero" for global warming because of the precedent they set for the rest of Canada.[27]

What becomes obvious in any discussion of the alternatives is that there is no silver bullet, and even the silver buckshot will have difficulty keeping up with demand in an oil supply–constrained future. BP exploration manager Richard Miller, in response to the statement about being saved by new technology, said that:

> This is the classical economist's view: something will turn up, when the price of oil is high enough, because something always does. But

there isn't anything conceivable that could replace conventional oil, in the same quantities or energy densities, at any meaningful price. We can't mine the oil sands in sufficient quantity because there isn't enough water to process them. We can't grow bio-fuels because there would be no land left to grow food. Solar, hydro, wind, and geothermal don't yield enough energy, hydrogen (from water) takes more energy to make than it can yield, and nuclear fission and fusion are presently off most political agendas. When oil gets too expensive, surviving Americans will still obtain energy from alternative sources, but in much smaller amounts and at much higher prices."[28]

The gap that is opening up between demand and supply will be equivalent to six thousand 500 megawatt power plants by 2030. None of the alternatives have the potential to get anywhere near being able to provide a reasonable proportion of this.

The UK minister for the environment from 1997 to 2003 Michael Meacher says, "Alternatives like biofuels, ethanol, or biomass can play a marginal role but nowhere near on the scale required. When the oil runs out the economic and social dislocation will be unprecedented." He goes on to quote Exxon Mobil's John Thompson who foresees that by 2015 we will need to find and develop eight out of the ten barrels of oil (and gas equivalent) from which we are now producing. This is just "not available," he concludes.[29]

In the United States there has been a growth in the interest in ethanol as the possible replacement for gasoline and biodiesel for diesel. The first-ever U.S. federal policy requiring steadily increasing levels of ethanol use, the Renewable Fuels Standard, was passed in July 2005 in the Energy Policy Act (HR 6). The RFS calls for an increasing amount of ethanol and biodiesel to be used nationwide between the years 2006 and 2012. The 2007 Energy Bill passed by the U.S. Congress calls for the production of 36 billion gallons of biofuels annually by 2022, an increase from approximately 7.5 billion gallons today.[30]

The number of flex-fuel vehicles (FFVs) (those able to consume ethanol) on the road in the U.S. makes up 2.4 percent of the vehicle fleet. And even with a jump in the number of gas stations offering ethanol, these still only make up 1 percent of U.S. gas stations. The energy bill mandates an increase in FFVs as well, but there is a long way to go before ethanol can contribute significantly to the yawning gap that is opening up between demand and supply.[31] Some motor vehicle

Box 2.1   Alternatives to Conventional Oil Extraction

Biofuels covers a broad category of fuels (solid, liquid, or gas) consisting of or derived from biological material or biomass. A popular example is ethanol, which is made from corn or sugar cane, and biodiesel from soybean and waste oil. These are promising but limited as discussed in more detail below.

Coal: While the use of coal is increasing in some countries, there is significant pressure to reduce coal use for environmental reasons. Coal is by far the worst greenhouse producer per unit of energy. In addition, new evidence is suggesting that "peak coal" may be a factor by 2025 due to the same practical limits that have been seen with oil and natural gas.[1]

Deepwater Drilling wells are generally considered to be those drilled in more than 1,000 feet of water. This method is often mentioned by oil companies as their solution, although it still requires considerable technological development to extract in a way that is economical. This is likely to happen as oil companies get better at finding oil (between 1996 and 2006, deepwater oil production rose more than eight times), but it will not bring back the age of cheap oil, and alone will not provide the answer to the oil shortage. As reported in MIT's *Technology Review*: "Although Chevron considers the 500-million-barrel Tahiti [deep water] field an 'elephant' of a find, for example, elephants aren't what they used to be. Saudi Arabia's Ghawar field, which was tapped in 1951, has already yielded some 54 billion barrels and may have 70 billion more. The U.S. alone, meanwhile, consumes roughly 20 million barrels of oil every day."[2]

"Dirty oil" extracted from tar sands and oil shale has serious environmental implications and requires huge amounts of water and natural gas to extract from sand and rock, making it a large greenhouse contributor. "To produce a barrel of synthetic crude through mining takes roughly eight hundred and ten megajoules, which is the energy content of about an eighth of a barrel of oil." This is also usually included as a real future option but is only a small contributor and will be hit hard by climate change restrictions.[3]

Electricity: Electric vehicles have been around for sometime and are likely to be a growing replacement for oil-based vehicles. Electric transit and small gopher electric vehicles are rapidly growing in use across the world as they are highly efficient (Tokyo's electric trains get 6,600 miles to the gallon). New plug-in electric cars and hybrids will be a growing option also. Electric options will grow rapidly if they are used as storage for renewables via a Smart Grid.[4]

GTL (gas-to-liquids) and CTL (coal-to-liquids) are tested technologies that have the potential to increase from their current small operations. But both require a significant amount of energy to create diesel, they are capital intensive, and the process emits significant greenhouse gases. The possible peaking of coal within 20 years suggests that coal to liquids is not going to be the answer.

Hydrogen requires an energy source to split it from water. It can then be used in hydrogen fuel-cell vehicles. This is not yet past the experimental phase in most vehicles, and widespread use would require a complete overhaul in infrastructure to make compressed hydrogen readily available. In the long term, hydrogen is a promising alternative fuel source as long as the process is powered by renewable sources.

1. David Strahan, www.guardian.co.uk/environment/2008/mar/05/ fossilfuels.energy.
2. Bryant Urstadt, "The Oil Frontier," *Technology Review*, Cambridge, MA: MIT, July 1, 2006.
3. Elizabeth Kolbert, "Unconventional Crude: Canada's Synthetic-Fuels Boom," *New Yorker*, November 12, 2007.
4. Chris Woodyard, "Tesla: Little electric roadster that could," *USA Today*, March 4, 2008, B1–2. (see pages 107 and 108)

manufacturers have chosen to make these FFVs as large gas-guzzling pickups and SUVs so they can increase the proportion of them in the market. As ethanol can only be found at 0.5 percent of gas stations (most of these being in the Upper Midwest) then FFVs are nearly all using gasoline; indeed many people don't even know they have FFVs. The Union of Concerned Scientists estimates that this policy on producing FFVs has *increased* gasoline consumption by 1.2 billion gallons or 1 percent.[32]

Biofuels have appeared to be an encouraging alternative, in part because of Brazil's success in distilling a growing proportion of their fuel from sugarcane. However, there is a growing chorus of voices, distressed by the growing conflict between food for people and food for cars. Lester Brown shows that grain reserves worldwide have been depleted by this sudden increase in use of U.S. corn for ethanol production, and that a doubling of this production (which seems almost certain) will induce a major crisis in the price of grain; this is occurring when nearly a billion people in the world remain malnourished. In 2008, a UN agency, the Food and Agriculture Organization, stated that "biofuel uses along with growing demand for food has pushed world food stocks to their lowest level since 1982." Traditional biofuels may have a role in agricultural regions as a fuel to assist farmers in their production but face many resource challenges as a widespread fuel for cities. Some potential does exist for converting cellulosic material (agricultural and forestry waste, for example) to ethanol.[33] As with many of the alternative fuel options, the production of biofuels results in considerable greenhouse gas emissions. Two studies published in the journal *Science* in 2008 found that investing in biofuels could cause severe environmental damage.[34] The only alternative that is showing any real potential is the Plug-in Hybrid Electric Vehicle (PHEV), based on renewable energy. The problem of fluctuation in the electricity grid from renewables (like PV, wind and wavepower) is solved by the storage capacity of PHEVs that can be charged at night (when grids shed power) and stabilize the grid during peak demand by receiving and releasing power. PHEVs and a Smart Grid offer a renewable solution to transport; though it will take 20 years to move a transport system into even a small proportion of such vehicles and such power systems.

This overview shows that there are some acceptable alternatives to petroleum fuels, but time is needed to determine how to invest in these alternatives in a manner that will not tax world food resources or result in increased greenhouse gas emissions.

The Petroleum Decline

The production cycle of petroleum fuels, conventional and nonconventional oil, and natural gas, is set out in figure 2.2. It is consistent with how we believe the depletion is likely to happen due to supply issues and will need to happen to meet targets for greenhouse gas reduction. This figure suggests that conventional oil peaking is occurring now and that this will ensure the price of oil remains high. It concedes that we have a few years of nonconventional oil and gas remaining. It points to a critical turning point around 2010 when even with all the deep water oil and natural gas on-stream, the global peak in petroleum will occur. The demand curve is set to grow but at a much lower rate than previous growth as the price of these fuels increases. However, all conventional projections have suggested the growth in demand is likely to continue in our cities and regions—though it just cannot be met by conventional supplies.

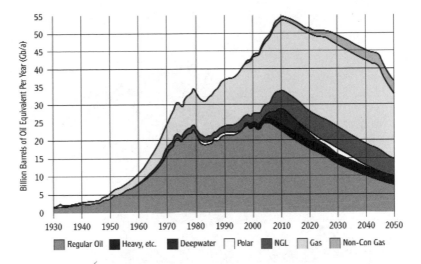

Figure 2.2 Global oil and natural gas production cycles according to ASPO.

In order to gather some perspective on the transition to the future it is important to see how we use fuels now and how each use is likely to change.

Diesel is presently used for small-scale power stations and for pumping water; these can now be easily replaced by solar and wind technologies and thus diesel for nontransport purposes should be rapidly phased out.[35] Some extra premium should be applied to diesel for ground freight, agriculture, and aviation as these would appear to be functions where there are direct economic benefits and where alternatives are not readily available (apart from biodiesel in agriculture, which should be feasible in some places). Heating oil is rapidly being replaced and has the potential to be phased out by refineries in favor of other grades of oil that can be applied to more premium uses. Gasoline, the biggest part of the oil pie, inevitably must enter a steep decline in use. Natural gas can take up only a small proportion of the transport and building task. The potential for alternative fuels to fill this looming gap between oil demand and oil production is set out in figure 2.3. As discussed earlier, we do not see the potential to replace more than half of the potential decline in oil supply with alternative fuel options. The focus of this book is on the large gap above the alternative fuels in figure 2.3. What can replace the increase in oil demand that has been driving the growth of our cities and regions? What will take up the slack as the decline of oil resources sets in? We look at this question in subsequent chapters.

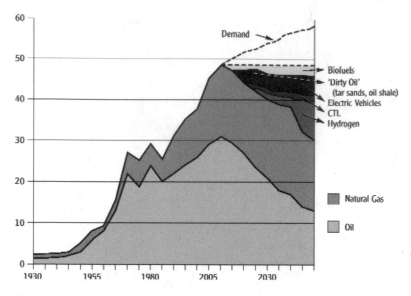

Figure 2.3 How alternative fuels could take up the slack as petroleum declines.

How Quickly Will We Decline?

Climate change imperatives suggest reductions in greenhouse gases of at least 50 percent by 2050, from around 9 GT of CO_2 to around 4.5 GT of CO_2 are needed worldwide.

Oil production is predicted to decline to approximately15 billion barrels a year by 2050; a 50 percent reduction. Remarkably the two agendas of climate change and peak oil overlap precisely: 50 percent less by 2050.

One is demand driven, the other is supply driven. Either way, we have to find a way to reduce the *need* for these fuels. For oil, it will mean designing cities in which we drive 25 to 50 percent less. Trucking will carry 25 to 50 percent less freight, and aviation will have even fewer planes. For our buildings it will mean 25 to 50 percent less fuel will be necessary for heating and cooling. Is this possible? What technologies will be needed to help make this happen? How will we rethink our cities to meet these goals?

These numbers challenge everything we do in our cities. They will require radical changes when all projections are for continued growth. While the challenge is indeed substantial, we suggest that overcoming it is feasible. The first step is awareness, and the second step is imagination.

Imagining how we can make substantial changes in the use of oil is daunting unless the change is made in small steps. To reduce our fossil fuel use 50 percent by 2050 requires just a 1.73 percent decline each year. On its face this doesn't seem very much. Can this really halve our use of fossil fuels by midcentury? It is of course the issue of exponential growth that masks the power in these numbers. For years environmentalists have been warning about the power of exponential growth in population and resource consumption to overwhelm our planet. Now exponential decline in fossil fuel resources can work in our favor as we are forced to plan for change. We are already seeing changes as we enter this new phase. For example, renewable energy (mostly wind and solar) is growing at around 40 percent per year.

In terms of resilience thinking, the challenge for our cities is to reduce petroleum fuels at a rate that can manage the global climate and peak oil agendas, but not destroy the social fabric of the city in the process. Responding to this challenge is necessary even if the oil and climate crisis were not happening, but it makes the agenda of managing the car and making more use of the sun even more vital, if not critical, to the future of cities.

Conclusion

There are serious questions about whether further expansion of cities is possible based on petroleum-dependent buildings and petroleum-dependent transportation. Even before the oil/climate crisis there were real limits setting in to the sprawl of cities, in part due to increased recognition of the economic, health, and environmental costs of sprawl. Now they must be accepted as the agenda that will define their future economies.

It is of course entirely feasible to imagine much worse futures than the one we have tried to lay out here with a simple 1.73 percent per annum decline in all fossil fuels. In the next chapter we will look at scenarios based on much larger declines in fuel availability that suddenly occur and cause social chaos. It will not be possible, for example, to have our cities adapt overnight to 5 or 10 percent cuts in supply without experiencing significant hardship. Thus it is essential that we begin the process of decarbonizing and reducing our dependence on petroleum in our cities as soon as possible. Building resilient, hopeful cities is needed to avoid a possible collapse due to their vulnerability from dependence on fossil fuels. In the next chapter we look at various scenarios depending on how cities respond to this challenge.

3

Four Scenarios for the Future of Cities: Collapse, Ruralized, Divided, or Resilient City

The response to the first oil crisis in the early 1970s varied from city to city across the globe. Our experiences described in the preface were mirrored by many. Two Washington transport public officials, Alan Pisarski and Neil De Terra, studied how European cities responded to the embargo and found weekend bans on driving as well as considerable increases in transit use. In the United States, however, they found that most people opted to stay at home and took fewer trips instead of shifting their mode of transport from the single-occupancy vehicle to walking, mass transit, biking, or car pooling. In many places the infrastructure was not in place for these alternative modes of travel. They concluded that for the United States "massive efforts were needed to advance the capacity and attractiveness of mass transit."[1]

In 2008 the response to skyrocketing gas prices has been quite different as mass transit systems in American cities have been overwhelmed by the surge in ridership. This response may differ from that of the 1973 embargo because the current situation is perceived as a longer-term problem rather than a temporary political situation, as well as the fact that there are many more mass transit options available. William W. Millar, president of the American Public Transportation Association, addressed the cause of this increase in ridership: "It's very clear that a significant portion of the increase in transit use is directly caused by people who are looking for alternatives to paying $3.50 for a gallon of gas."[2]

The current popular and political response to climate change and peak oil is to talk about clean energy and energy security by increasing local biofuel and oil supplies with some emphasis on making vehicles more efficient. President Bush (formerly employed by his family's oil company) announced in the 2006 State of the Union Address that "We are addicted to oil." He then went on to stress the need for more alternative fuels such as ethanol, but later expressed his support for opening restricted wilderness areas to oil exploration and lifting the ban on deep-sea drilling off the coasts of Florida and California. The United States still lacks a serious strategy to ease its addiction to oil.

Indeed, as noted in the previous chapter, some of the solutions are making things worse: new methods of production are increasing greenhouse gas emissions, some fuel-saving rules are being used to increase the number of gas-guzzling SUVs, and alternative fuels are driving up corn prices and depleting food sources. It is when concerned people discover this kind of information that they begin to lose hope. The other disheartening factor is that we are not learning from history. The lessons of the 1973–74 oil embargo and subsequent oil shocks have been quickly forgotten, as Pisarski and De Terra concluded about the U.S. response compared to European responses: "Rarely had the public so rapidly rushed back to 'normalcy' after a jarring event." They went on "We have put our faith in programs to increase exports and energy supplies, and the root problems in energy demands go unchallenged. On such a treadmill our goals will continue to elude us."[3]

Fuel prices will fluctuate but the constraints on oil are growing. If we do not have a broad strategy to address this when real scarcity sets in a panic response is all that remains, and Jared Diamond's scenario may not be far off:

> Thus, because we are rapidly advancing along this non-sustainable course, the world's environmental problems will get resolved, in one way or another, within the lifetimes of the children and young adults alive today. The only question is whether they will become resolved in pleasant ways of our own choice, or in unpleasant ways not of our choice, such as warfare, genocide, starvation, disease, epidemics, and collapses of societies."[4]

This book suggests we do have the ability to change the course of our cities and create resiliency rather than risk collapse, but we must take seriously the possibility that our response may not be sufficient or timely to avert some of the less-than-attractive scenarios set out below. While we introduce the option of resiliency in this chapter, reaching resiliency is discussed at greater length in the remaining chapters of the book.

Scenario 1: Collapse

We do not like to think about cities collapsing, but history is littered with fallen cities. Ephesus, in modern-day Turkey, was the second largest city in the Roman Empire. A thriving port city, it was abandoned in A.D. 1,000 when it could no longer function as a port due to the river silting up because the trees in the surrounding hills were all removed. Ephesus did not see the link between its environmental mismanagement, war, and its economy, but today you can walk in the ruins of a once great city port that used to be on the Mediterranean coast but is now five miles inland due to erosion. A similar series of stories can be found in the Bible with cities like Babylon (see resilientcitiesbook.org).

Jared Diamond defines collapse as "a drastic decrease in human population size and/or political/economic/social complexity over a considerable area, for an extended time." He goes on to say that collapses are "an extreme form of several milder types of decline."[5]

The language of collapse is largely confined to anthropology, archeology, ancient history, ecology, or theology. We will cross these disciplines as we think about whether our cities and rural regions can address this deep challenge of resource scarcity and what will likely emerge. But in the end the analysis must depend on the fundamental values and views of society.[6]

The eminent scientist James Lovelock, who first saw the issue of CFCs in the atmosphere and who has tantalized the world with his theories of Gaia (how the earth functions as a super-organism), believes that climate change is now irreversible and that by the end of the century human population will be reduced from 7 billion to 500 million. He believes that by 2020 we will see the start of extreme weather, and then collapse will begin:

> By 2040, the Sahara will be moving into Europe, and Berlin will be as hot as Baghdad. Atlanta will end up a kudzu jungle. Phoenix will become uninhabitable, as will parts of Beijing (desert), Miami (rising seas) and London (floods). Food shortages will drive millions of people north, raising political tensions. The Chinese have nowhere to go but up into Siberia. With hardship and mass migrations will come epidemics, which are likely to kill millions.[7]

In 2005 the world watched in amazement as the city of New Orleans collapsed due to an extreme climate event. The lack of preparation in the

Ephesus collapsed in 1000 A.D. after its port was silted up from excessive cutting of forests in its bioregion. It is now five miles inland. (Credit: iStock.com)

city was scandalous. Once all civilizing constraints disappeared people tried desperately to find food and safety. The scenes shocked us all. But history suggests that we shouldn't be shocked—the potential is there in any city. Lewis Mumford talked about Necropolis as the city which is destined to collapse and described its characteristics: " . . . above all, the massive collective concentration on glib ephemeralities of all kinds. . . . When these signs multiply, Necropolis is near, though not a stone has yet crumbled." After all the pain and death of collapse, we attempt to re-build such cities and sometimes learn from the lessons. New Orleans has spawned a whole industry of people reflecting on its lessons.[8]

Commentators like Jacob Bronowski in *The Ascent of Man*, see the growth of cities and industrial change as a continually upward journey that brings more and more knowledge with all its potential to create a better world. Other commentators like Paul Ehrlich, Ted Trainer, and Bill Mollison argue that urbanization took us on a downward journey in which we began to lose contact with the earth, to pollute and degrade it, and to create bigger and bigger cities where people became more and more alienated. The history outlined above suggests that both ideas are likely to have some truth. But neither group would posit that collapse should be contemplated or accepted.[9]

The questions about peak oil and climate change are answered by "climate doomsayers" and the "peakers" with an increasingly apocalyptic tinge. They do not believe that the opportunities for creating resilient cities outlined in this book are possible. They believe that in an age of oil consumption there will be continued growth in automobile dependency, sprawling suburbs, and poorly designed buildings. They believe that our cities and rural regions will find the transition to a post-oil economy very difficult; indeed they see the potential for full scale collapse due to the lack of any real response while there is still time.

When a survey on the Web site oilcrisis.com asked "experts" "What next?," they could only envision collapse. Colin Campbell for example describes a "crumbling stock market" and "one of the greatest economic and political discontinuities of all time." Les Magoon from the U.S. Geological Survey says "hang on tight . . . it's going to be quite a ride."[10] David Lankshear and Neil Cameron suggest that:

> The cost of everything that depends on oil will rise. Airlines will become unaffordable to the average citizen and will go bankrupt as a result. Once the airlines stop flying the world's largest employer, international tourism will take a severe economic hit. Smaller nations dependent on tourism will become bankrupt. The flow-on effects of oil prices skyrocketing out of control will throw us into the Greater Depression.[11]

Yet this is one of the milder scenarios suggested. A rash of Web sites hint at some of the worst nightmares imaginable (see, for example, www.lifeaftertheoilcrash.net; www.dieoff.com). Republican congressman Roscoe Bartlett, after discovering peak oil in March 2005, said in Congress "Civilization as we know it will end soon." Like most new movements there is a good deal of overstatement in the rhetoric of peakers. They emphasize the problem and have few solutions as they feel the most important issue is to raise awareness. Peakers are suggesting that we should be preparing for a major depression if not a collapse of our cities and rural regions.

David Holmgren, one of the originators of the permaculture concept, is one of the few to venture into what he calls speaking at the "God level"; he describes the collapse as the "die-off scenario":

> The die-off scenario is actually the whole end to the development of intensive, settled agriculture, civilization and industrialization—all of

the last 6,000 years swept into the dustbin of history. What goes with that is a very large drop in human population in a relatively short time, like 100 years—possibly back to some sort of hunter-gatherer type of organization, with a much depleted resource level and without the capacity to use the resources we can use now.[12]

Serious oil shortages could lead to panic and social collapse on a large scale. Even a slow decline in oil can unleash forces that are barely imaginable in our cities as the people who have little flexibility in their household income increasingly have to spend a higher and higher proportion of their money for transport fuel and for household power and fuel. With the subprime mortgage meltdown in the United States, increasing oil prices are invoking panic. Michael Rose from the Energy Desk at Angus Jackson says "With the credit crisis going on, everyone is on edge and the slightest disruption in crude oil or its products takes prices right up."[13]

The subprime mortgage crisis also shows how whole areas of a city can collapse in a relatively short time. In his 2008 *Atlantic Monthly* article "The Next Slum?" Chris Leinberger of the Brookings Institution chronicles some of the suburban decay brought on by the subprime mortgage crisis: "In the first half of last year, residential burglaries rose by 35 percent and robberies by 58 percent in suburban Lee County, Florida, where one in four houses stands empty. Charlotte's crime rates have stayed flat overall in recent years—but from 2003 to 2006, in the 10 suburbs of the city that have experienced the highest foreclosure rates, crime rose 33 percent."[14]

Many residents who moved to the suburbs seeking cheaper housing are unable to adjust their budgets or lifestyles when faced with skyrocketing oil prices. The options for switching to transit or walking are often not feasible, alternative heating options are not available, and vehicles cannot be fueled.

Widespread anxiety can rapidly lead to panic and fear as opportunities for adaptation disappear. In Diamond's scenarios it was denial about the future that led to those societies' inability to cope with change. Under the influence of this panic, institutions like banks can collapse as mortgages are not paid. Cities can absorb a certain amount of strain as people move and stay with families or support institutions. However, there comes a point where people's desperation causes the resilience of civil society to be undermined. At this point people start leaving and those who cannot leave live in fear. This is followed by the loss of law and order until eventually all the support structures of government are withdrawn. All of the food, water, waste, and health systems we rely on begin to collapse. The generally unspoken part of this scenario is widespread dispersion and death as support structures collapse everywhere. "We have to be careful not to rush from denial to despair," says John Elkington an environmental consultant in London.[15]

It is of course hard to believe that complete collapse of civilization is a realistic scenario, though collapse cannot be underestimated in the vast suburban areas of many cities that grew with cheap oil and may die with its demise. But as will be shown, in oil-dependent cities, options for vulnerable areas are being sought and awareness among concerned sections of society is growing rapidly. Whether these changes are happening fast enough is most uncertain. Indeed the "early adopters" cities are showing what can be achieved in planning to avoid collapse (as outlined in chapters 4, 5, and 6).

Scenario 2: Ruralized City

One of the most significant transitions in human history was from a hunter-gatherer society to an agricultural-urban society—the Neolithic revolution as it is known to science. This occurred sometime around 13,500 years ago in the Middle East after the Ice Age when certain grain crops began to be farmed rather than gathered and certain animals began to be domesticated. The great significance for humanity and for the discussion here is that both changes allowed settlements to be built around fertile river valleys. Cities were born out of their agricultural settlements and have a close synergy with the production systems in their bioregion.[16]

Once people began to grow and graze what they wanted they could create a surplus in good times and store it. This released some people from the daily task of finding their own food and enabled them to manage settlements and create new technologies. A whole range of human opportunity was thus created. The processes of urban civilization were made possible when people left the "garden" of nature and began creating human settlements. Human history shows many hunter-gatherer societies existed across the world. They were, and still are in some cases, highly ingenious in taking from nature what they need to survive without destroying it. The Neolithic Revolution in the Americas began seven to eight thousand years after it began in the Middle East. However, whenever people have come into contact with a society that is settled, with agricultural surpluses and technologies of cities, they have chosen to come out of Eden.[17]

Although we dream of more utopian pasts, history tells us that the process is one way—we cannot return. From approximately ten thousand years ago, when the world became warmer and drier, many of these first Middle Eastern settlements did collapse as their ecological base was ruined. These societies then spread west and east from the Fertile Crescent, and as the climate warmed created the settlements and agricultural areas in Europe and Asia as we know them today. Some of the new settlements also collapsed as they depleted their soils or were unable to manage their settlements or were destroyed by invaders.[18]

But at no stage did the people in these cities go back to Eden, to the hunter-gatherer existence. The broad sweep of history shows that cities tend to be rebuilt and have endured and grown rather than people ever becoming hunter-gatherers again, despite the sometimes romantic appeal of "rewilding."[19]

One of the key ideas being presented as a response to peak oil is that our cities will create a more sustainable semi-rural lifestyle, and each city will be responsible for producing a large proportion of its own food. This is seen to be a kind of suburban agriculture based on permaculture or hobby farms. In this scenario most needs are met locally and the economy is devolved down to the individual household primarily, or to small groups. Heating is provided by wood grown locally and there is little need to travel as needs are met locally by a far more self-sufficient economy. It is a ruralization of cities, somewhat akin to medieval society but with a strongly individualistic flavor.[20]

David Holmgren, for example, sees the suburbs as a farming opportunity waiting to happen:

> "Suburban sprawl" in fact gives us an advantage. Detached houses are easy to retrofit, and the space around them allows for solar access and space for food production. A water supply is already in place, our pampered, unproductive ornamental gardens have fertile soils and ready access to nutrients, and we live in ideal areas with mild climates, access to the sea, the city and inland country.[21]

There are two problems with this approach. First, it provides a new rationale for urban sprawl that will consume land and other natural resources and will seriously undermine the future resiliency of cities.[22]

Urban sprawl based around isolated blocks is justified by permaculturalists as being sustainable due to its food production potential. (Credit: Timothy Beatley)

Second, it is distracting us from seeking region-wide solutions to these issues of energy, water, waste, and food production in favor of individualized approaches, which may not be equitable. Cities are collective entities and should solve their problems through common good solutions to avoid the risk of becoming highly exclusive. For those people and parts of the city unable to create food and manage water and wastes through permaculture, the future in a ruralized city would be very bleak.

The population in this scenario is often reduced many fold to enable a more sustainable level. In this scenario the population of Australia is expected to drop to 1 or 2 million and the world to 1 or 2 billion, presumably through premature deaths.[23]

The transition is often discussed with some relish on the Web as the antipopulation, antiurban movements often link together to imagine a ruralized city as the preferred future to achieve their objectives of people living closer to nature and avoiding the problems of a globalized economy. Peak oil is thus sometimes grabbed hold of with glee as the means to obtain this vision of the ruralized city.[24]

In some ways this apocalyptic view, which sees peak oil leading to a painful "revolution" before leading to the dawn of a new rural age of harmony, is similar to a Marxist or communist view of history. In this view revolutionary collapse is seen as inevitable due to the laws of ecology and thermodynamics, and now the laws of oil depletion curves. From these ashes a new kind of idealized rural utopia will emerge. Mao and Pol Pot certainly thought this way was the only morally correct lifestyle.

We do not believe that a return to a fully rural or hunter-gatherer lifestyle is a desirable outcome or that it is likely to happen. We do not believe that individualized permaculture in vast sprawling suburbs will take over the role of cities. But are there positive aspects to ruralizing a city?

A whole array of eco-village experiments have emerged as potential models for how rural areas can be productive and sustainable (see the Global Eco-Village Network, gen.ecovillage.org). They are now moving into cities with eco-village experiments like those in Ithaca, New York, Los Angeles , and Somerville, Western Australia. Eco-villages are intentional communities, in an urban or rural setting, in which the residents share social, environmental, and economic goals. The creation of these communities has led to some wonderful innovations in small-scale technology and community governance.[25] The question is where should such a community fit in the new city?

There is no doubt that urban eco-villages have a role in the resilient city. However, it is a specialized role, one for people who are committed to a more communal life and one where there is a strong emphasis on self-sufficiency. There is a tradition of agriculture within cities, and potential for urban agriculture to provide a substantial proportion of the city's food needs, most notably in the Third World. But it is not the primary function of the city, even in those cities that are seen to be doing urban agriculture well, such as cities in Cuba. Those who want to ruralize the city seem to want food production to be its main function. Food production should be available to residents of cities through many different means such as roof gardens, allotments, community gardens, and backyards (as set out in chapter 4) and through eco-villages specifically designed for urban areas. However, this agricultural production should not be the primary function of the city.[26]

There are other rural functions that could be brought more directly into the city of the future. Cities will need to be more closely connected to the creation of renewable energy, the provision of water, and the processing of wastes. These are moving inexorably into smaller-scale technologies that can fit more easily into cities and thus will be much more energy efficient. However, they must be constructed as a common good function to create an equitable society. The elderly, the poor, and the

Ithaca Eco-Village has developed into an urban eco-village, which is now contributing to city sustainability through its community-based approaches: a communal food storage area requiring no artificial heating or cooling (top) and community housing (bottom). (Credit: Peter Newman)

disabled cannot be expected to produce their own food and energy, collect their own water, or recycle their own waste. Contributions should be made by every household.[27] Some high-rise commercial buildings are now fulfilling a substantial proportion of their own energy needs, collecting rain water to use in toilets (even mining the sewer for this purpose), and significantly reducing the waste produced from construction and operations. (The green building revolution is discussed in chapter 4.) But in their dense city centers, these buildings still need to be part of the grid system. While a movement is emerging to reuse vacant lots for growing food, there are limited opportunities for this in the densely developed parts of cities. On the other hand, these centers are where traditional urban functions are concentrated and where transit and walking are feasible due to the densities. This conflict between the need for density to solve the brown problem of urban sustainability and the need for space to solve the green problem of urban sustainability is a real issue. It is suggested that the peri-urban areas between and at the end of the more urban corridors can be phased into being more rural (with the reductions in oil causing these areas to be no longer viable as car-dependent fringe suburbs); when this happens, it is possible to imagine a whole array of urban eco-villages colonizing the space. In these places much of a city's renewable energy could be produced; much of a city's waste could be mined, treated, and recycled using the clever technologies of the Sixth Wave (see below); and some of the city's specialized food needs could be produced there. This kind of ruralization of the city seems not only plausible but desirable. However, it is not the same as the vision that some have for ruralizing the city, through self-sustaining households, which we believe will be unsustainable for the entire city.

Followers of permaculture are familiar with the example set by Cuban cities. Heinberg writes about how Cuba was forced to adapt to living with almost no oil after 1989 with the collapse of the Soviet Union, which had provided them with fuel. With mainly dense, walkable settlements that require little car use, the cities were relatively resilient in this period. But they also began to take on a bigger role in food production, particularly vegetables, which were grown in every conceivable piece of ground in and around the city. Some gardens are on roof tops but most are in peri-urban locations close to the city. Vegetable production in the city grew to provide 45 percent of the total consumed, thus cutting back on oil used for transport while enabling people to have very fresh vegetables.[28]

The cities in Cuba have retained their primary urban functions while increasing their role in vegetable production. Cities in history have produced vegetables in market gardens. Paris in the early nineteenth century was said to be an exporter of vegetables grown in market gardens on manure from its horses. Chinese cities continue to have this function close to their intensely urban activities. Market gardens have been part of cities since they began, and even today the world's big cities have many peri-urban functions related to food production. This is a function that cities everywhere can and should reclaim much more intensively.

The agricultural city idea has been proposed for Detroit as the population of the urban core has continued to decline. "It may be that the future of Detroit lies in a series of viable communities linked by open spaces, parks, forests, and farms," states Professor Roy Strickand, director of the Masters in Urban Design program at the University of Michigan.[29] We would suggest that this rural agenda needs to be integrated into a parallel urban revitalization agenda if Detroit is to become a more resilient city.

The wonders of science and all the best human ingenuity and creativity will be needed to make our cities and rural regions work better, to come to grips with our degradation of resources—but it will still be an imaginable city, not a rural utopia—we have left Eden. While our bioregions will need to develop a better synergy with our cities, they should not usurp them.

Peak oil poses a genuine challenge to our cities and their regions. However, this need not mean the collapse of our urban society, nor should we contemplate the ruralized city as an antiurban process of deconstructing our cities; at worst this is a serious misdirection and at best a distraction. The distraction will prevent us from fully acknowledging the extent of the possibility of collapse and instead will allow totally unsustainable, oil-dependent, rural-oriented suburbs to continue to be built. An urban eco-village expression of this ruralized city could, however, have some advantages, and parts of cities should be dedicated to this function.

Scenario 3: Divided City

In the divided city scenario the wealthy recognize that they need to optimize their choices and begin to form exclusive neighborhoods and self-sufficient centers with all the best transit and walkability. They will have all necessary services within a short distance and all institutions for supporting such centers available locally. Likewise all the best solar design and renewable technology will be built into these exclusive areas. As the threat of oil scarcity begins to bite they will retreat more and more inside these eco-enclaves, guarding their rights with fences, guard dogs, and arms—or the biggest barrier of all—real estate prices.

The poor will be left with cheap housing on the urban fringe and very few services or opportunities for transit. Heating and other building energy will remain dependent on oil and gas or whatever can be found. Alternative technologies, alternative transport, and alternative locations will be unaffordable. Businesses will collapse as they will be too far away for workers to reach. As the double whammy of climate change restrictions on fossil fuels and the petroleum supply crisis strikes, these areas will collapse. These auto-dependent areas will quickly become crime-ridden. The *Mad Max* movie series was created by George Miller to dramatize the peak oil issue. In these stories people descend into lawlessness and gang-based domination, with gasoline as the key commodity for survival. Civil wars in these areas (as in the developing world) are the scenes of considerable suffering and premature loss of life despite the resources of the rich who are safely ensconced nearby. This is a city full of fear.

James Lovelock says, "We can return to a more primitive lifestyle and live in equilibrium with the planet as hunter-gatherers, or we can sequester ourselves in a very sophisticated, high-tech civilization."[30] In this scenario the future may belong to the few who are lucky enough to buy or fight their way into the exclusive eco-enclaves that will characterize our cities.

Could this be our future? Unfortunately there are signs that this is already happening. Many countries have had divided cities, but even in some South African cities we are seeing forces of hope.[31]

The first signs of the self-sufficient enclaves appeared in the form of gated communities in the 1980s and can also be seen emerging in some New Urbanist developments.

The New Urbanist agenda (which conceptually is totally allied to the approach taken in this book) calls for walkable, higher density, mixed-use communities. These communities, generally, are highly desirable and can become exclusive as they appeal to people who want to live more sustainably and usually have the means to afford it. While the New Urbanists have addressed affordable housing in collaborating with the U.S. government on HOPE VI (an effort to rebuild blighted public housing

A gated community in Los Angeles complete with armed guards. (Credit: Peter Newman)

projects to be high-density, mixed income, and walkable), there are few examples of successful mixed-income, New Urbanist projects built in walkable urban locations with transit. Many highly sought after developments are now stressing their reduced car dependence, solar architecture, and other ecological features.[32]

The polarization of different populations within cities has long been an area of academic study. Throughout most of the past few hundred years urban areas have attracted the rural poor as they offer new opportunities while these prospects dwindle in rural areas. The urban poor may have had comparative poverty in relation to others in the city, but they were almost always better off as urban poor than as rural poor as they have greater access to resources in urban areas. In the divided city scenario, the poor populations would remain in semi-rural areas on the urban fringe, as it would be too expensive for them to move to a more urban area. The wealthy would live in walkable, mixed-use urban communities with access to jobs and amenities. The semi-rural poor would remain dependent on diminishing amounts of oil for transportation. There are many global cities that already demonstrate this kind of division between the urban enclave for the rich and the slum on the fringe of the city for the poor.[33]

The evidence of the poor becoming more and more isolated on the car-dependent urban fringe is very clear in Australia and increasingly so in North America as the focus of social policy has been on creating affordable housing on cheap land. The emphasis has not been on creating affordable housing in urban areas that is walkable, transit accessible, and energy efficient. New housing is generally considered to be affordable if it requires no more than 30 percent of a household income. However, in 2005 over one third of American households were spending more than this on housing. Also, traditional accounting of housing costs does not include transportation expenses, so living in the outlying suburbs, when compared to today's higher-priced urban center, seems like a bargain. But true housing costs (separate from environmental costs) need to consider household expenditures on transportation, especially in the age of diminishing oil supplies.[34]

A 2006 study by the Brookings Institution Center for Neighborhood Technology and Center for Transit-Oriented Development shows how widely the transportation costs may vary according to location: "Nationally, transportation is the second largest household expenditure after housing, ranging from less than 10 percent of the average household's expenditures in transit-rich areas to nearly 25 percent in many other areas." (The study is part of a new tool offered to measure the true affordability of housing choices.) In 2006, the average household spent 34 percent of its income on housing, and the second largest expenditure was transportation at 18 percent. If oil prices continue to rise then the social collapse in the vast car-dependent suburbs around cities like Atlanta and Houston will accelerate while compact cities and parts of cities with diverse and resilient alternative transport options will be resilient.[35]

How will the world accommodate high-fuel-consuming cities? For those who believe in the divided city scenario, it is highly improbable that oil will be shared to accommodate those who need it most. We are likely to see the reverse of the situation in America in the 1960s as those who could afford to fled to the suburbs. Those with sufficient wealth will move to those cities or parts of the city where there are opportunities to live better with less oil. The divided city will increasingly exist through forced electronic and armed security. It is a city of fear.

A form of the divided city scenario can be seen in industrial cities such as Detroit and Philadelphia in the United States and Liverpool,

England. Liverpool very nearly totally collapsed when the population dropped to 1920 levels and over 70 percent of its remaining occupants were on some form of benefit. Detroit and Philadelphia similarly had huge population loss as their traditional manufacturing base moved overseas and they were not able to adapt quickly enough to the new information economy. All three cities became highly divided. Those who participated in what remained of the old manufacturing economy were extremely well off, and those who did not lived in poverty and squalor. Entire communities were faced with no employment possibilities and those remaining were left to survive on their wits and on welfare—both being insufficient. All three cities have begun to turn this around through emphasizing different futures for their urban areas.[36]

Disparities in availability and shortages in oil have been and continue to be the basis of wars between cities and between nations (Japan was cut off from global oil supplies leading up to World War II). If cities don't respond then oil wars may well go on.

If the future is left to short-term market interests it will lead rapidly to the divided city. A long-term perspective and incremental strategic planning are required to help shape markets in the transition away from oil. Long-term issues that challenge us with the prospect of collapse bring out deeper fears and feed into the divided city mentality. Thus it is necessary to get going quickly on the demonstrations of hope that can help people see how a resilient city can be built instead.

Scenario 4: Resilient City

The resilient city scenario occurs when the access and alternate forms of fuel and buildings in eco-enclaves that were the province of the wealthy in the divided city scenario are provided for all. People will have access to jobs and services by transit or walking as well as the use of electric cars for short car journeys. Intercity movements will move toward fast electric rail and will be reduced considerably by the new generation high quality interactive video conferencing. Green building design and renewable fuels will be a part of all neighborhoods. The city will develop new rail links to all parts of the city, walkable centers will be created across the city-region using the best green buildings and infrastructure. In the areas between the intensively developed transit centers and corridors, urban eco-villages will be established to help manage the city's ecological functions such as extra renewable energy production and water and waste recycling; these will be linked into a citywide green infrastructure system through clever control systems and local management. Urban eco-villages will also grow specialized agricultural produce and manage areas of urban biodiversity; they will be largely self-sufficient though they will still be within reasonable distance of the city for many urban functions.

In the rural regions around cities most agricultural and forestry production will focus on food and fiber and biofuels for the city and its region, thus reducing food and fiber miles. The manufacturing of products will become more localized and be more biologically based to replace petrochemicals. The towns where goods are produced will be well linked by freight rail to the city. Mining and tourism similarly will cut back significantly in the amount of fuel the industries use and there will be a shift toward more local employment, natural gas and then hydrogen with the investment in new technology (such as new-generation air ships that use one-tenth of the fuel of planes and can glide quietly over regional and remote areas).

These are not simple changes, however, and there is little question that the transition will be difficult. This transition has been referred to as the Sixth Wave of industrialism because it is a complete reorientation of industrial society to a different set of technologies and a rethinking of how we organize cities. Each of the waves is distinct in the technology introduced and the form the city has taken (see figure 3.5).[37]

The First Wave cities were traditional walking cities with some use of horses and carriages while new industries began to develop along rivers and canals using water power. The Second Wave cities spread out along the railways of the steel and steam era. European cities have retained much of this corridor form. The Third Wave of electricity and the internal combustion engine saw electric tramways built, especially in the burgeoning cities of America such as Los Angeles, which had the world's most extensive tramway system. These cities followed linear development patterns along the tramways. At the same time the first cars and buses were appearing though they did not begin to shape city form until the Fourth Wave, which was dominated by cheap oil and which enabled cities to spread and sprawl in every direction. Thus was created the automobile city that confronts us today with the challenge of fossil fuel reduction. The Fifth Wave of Internet and digital technologies has replaced the old industrial manufacturing centers of cities with knowledge jobs, thus helping to minimize some of the sprawl and spur the re-

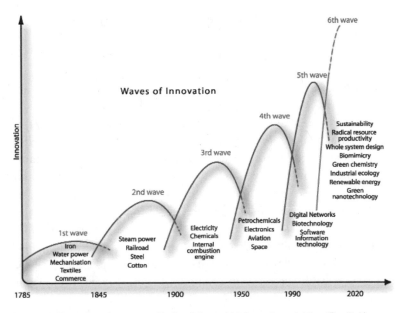

Figure 3.5 The successive waves of industrialism which have shaped cities. (Credit: Hargroves and Smith, 2005.)

newal of these older industrial sites. However the Fifth Wave still had cheap oil enabling cars to further dominate cities.

The Sixth Wave coincides with the end of cheap oil. It is the beginning of an era of resource productivity and investment in a new series of sustainability technologies related to renewables and distributed, small-scale water, energy, and waste systems (building on clever control systems and Smart Grids now perfected from the Fifth Wave), all of which are more local and require far less fuel to distribute.

This all means the city can become much more polycentric. The transport systems that support such polycentricity appear to be new electric transit systems for fast cross-city movement and a series of small-scale electric and hybrid vehicles for small local trips as well as walking and cycling, which have survived all the city form changes. The polycentric centers and the remaining suburban buildings all need to be renewed with solar and other eco-technologies of the Sixth Wave. It is clear that the changes needed for the resilient city are not just technology substitutions, they are in the business paradigms, the culture of the utilities that will provide the infrastructure, and the organization that can enable new ways of managing our cities; every householder needs to be part of it.

The resilient city will require changes at all levels of our urban economies.

Conclusions

The four scenarios laid out are all possible outcomes of diminishing oil supplies and a necessary response to recognition of the impact of cities on climate change. It is quite clear that our sympathies lie with a transition to the resilient city, which is the only option that will protect the natural amenities needed to support life on the planet, will not be vulnerable to oil shortages and carbon taxes, and will be equitable. Collapse is obviously not a compelling option; the ruralized city based on individualized permaculture is likely to destroy and consume more natural resources as lower-density communities spread out, and could easily result in more battles over existing resources; and the divided city discounts the welfare of all but the wealthy.

The past few hundred years of industrialism should give us some sense that we have adapted successfully and can do it again. It is the great experiment in retaining cities of hope. The resilient city scenario is not a soft option; it is the only option that we should be contemplating, as in the end it is the only option based on hope. So the question is, How do we get started on this new journey?

4

A Vision for Resilient Cities:
The Built Environment

What does a resilient city look like? Bike paths and virtually car-free streets that lead from solar homes to grocery stores, recreation areas, parks, or a free tram to reach places too far to walk or bike. A solar office block filled with new Sixth Wave businesses. Schools with parents lined up on bikes to pick up kids instead of waiting in idling cars. A local farmers market for buying bioregional produce.

This is a common scene in Vauban, a development of five thousand households on a former military base in Freiburg, Germany. Vauban is considered a model ecological community that is being studied with increasing interest as the economic, health, and environmental costs of car dependence come into focus.[1] Residents are offered numerous incentives (such as free tram passes and options for carpooling) and disincentives (extremely pricey parking only available on the edge of town) to live car free. (There is already a strong disincentive to driving with gas over eight U.S. dollars per gallon.) The car ownership rate in Vauban is 150 vehicles per 1,000 inhabitants, compared to the U.S. average of 640 vehicles per 1,000 residents.[2]

How does a city achieve resiliency? The positive examples that illuminate the steps toward resiliency described below have been achieved by a mixture of visionary grassroots initiatives demanding more options for sustainable living and transport, innovative business, and strong political leadership offering incentives or regulating for more livable, sustainable environments from the regional to the building level.

In the previous chapters we outlined some overarching themes of the resilient city. Below we specify the seven key elements of a resilient city in the built environment that flow from these themes.

1. *Renewable Energy City.* Urban areas will be powered by renewable energy technologies from the region to the building level.

Vauban is a car-free eco-village that is setting new standards for sustainable urbanism and solar power. Shown above are the plus-energy homes that produce more energy than they need. (Credit: CABE/Alex Ely)

2. *Carbon Neutral City.* Every home, neighborhood, and business will be carbon neutral.

3. *Distributed City.* Cities will shift from large centralized power, water, and waste systems to small-scale and neighborhood-based systems.

4. *Photosynthetic City.* The potential to harness renewable energy and provide food and fiber locally will become part of urban green infrastructure.

5. *Eco-Efficient City.* Cities and regions will move from linear to circular or closed-loop systems, where substantial amounts of their energy and material needs are provided from waste streams.

6. *Place-Based City.* Cities and regions will understand renewable energy more generally as a way to build the local economy and nurture a unique and special sense of place.

7. *Sustainable Transport City.* Cities, neighborhoods, and regions will be designed to use energy sparingly by offering walkable, transit-oriented options for all supplemented by electric vehicles.

The Seven Elements of the Paradigm Shift to Resilient Cities

While no one city has shown innovation in all seven areas, some are quite advanced in one or two. The challenge will be to apply all of the resilient city characteristics together, to generate a sense of hope through a combination of new technology, city design, and community-based innovation.

The Renewable Energy City: Urban areas powered by renewable energy technologies from the region to the building level

The shift away from fossil-fuel dependency will require much greater levels of commitment from cities themselves—from the local governments and municipalities, large and small, that make up metropolitan areas. This influence can be considerable, especially in large cities, and where localities join together.

This requires that cities recognize, for instance, the links between transport and solar energy. All of our transport decisions and investments should be seen as opportunities to invest in renewables and to move cities in the direction of low oil dependence. For example, Calgary Transit's creative initiative "Ride the Wind" provides all the power needed for its light rail system from wind turbines in the south of Alberta. Given the importance of transportation in minimizing our oil dependence and our impact on climate change, transportation is addressed separately in the last step in this chapter and in the entire next chapter.

While some solar city projects are underway (including Masdar City in the Persian Gulf, which broke ground in 2008), presently no major cities in the world are powered entirely by renewable energy. A new development in Perth called North Port Quay with 10,000 dwellings plans to be completely carbon free (see www.northportquay.com.au).

Strong political support is needed to create the infrastructure for solar and wind power at the scale necessary to help power a city. While finding locations for large wind farms near urban areas has been controversial (such as the wind farm proposal that was defeated off the coast of Cape Cod, Massachusetts), there are significant opportunities to harness solar and wind power.

In 2005 researchers at Stanford University created a wind map to locate the most effective and efficient places for wind farms and found that North America has the greatest potential to harness this energy source. They also found that some of the strongest winds were in Northern Europe along the North Sea, the southern tip of South America, and the Australian island of Tasmania where winds are strong and sustained enough at the turbine blade height to create significant power.[3] The U.S. Department of Energy reported that by 2030 wind could power approximately 20 percent of the electrical grid in the United States (it is currently responsible for approximately one percent), resulting in a 25 percent drop in carbon emissions.[4] There are also new studies on how wind around buildings within cities can be tapped in small-scale power systems. Researcher Cristina Archer said, "The main implication of this study is that wind, for low-cost wind energy, is more widely available than was previously recognized."[5]

Hydropower has been used in cities such as Vancouver, British Columbia, and Christchurch, New Zealand, for decades. Few people see much more potential for hydropower due to the impact of large dams, but the role of geothermal power appears to be offering a similar level of base load renewable power.

A handful of cities around the world participated in a world solar city conference in 2001 and shared initiatives and goals to becoming a "solar city." Examples include Capetown, South Africa's, Integrated Metropolitan Environmental Policy (IMEP), which has an energy strategy designed to put the city in the lead "in meeting energy needs in a sustainable way where everyone has access to affordable and healthy energy services, where energy is used efficiently, and where transport is efficient, equitable, and emphasizes public transport and compact planning." The goals include 10 percent of the energy supply coming from renewable sources by 2020. Other cities like Adelaide, in the state of South Australia, have gone from 0 to 20 percent renewable energy in ten years by building four large wind farms.[6]

Another renewable city example is Daegu, Korea, which is developing a master plan that will result in the integration of renewable energy into city development. The city established the Center for Solar City Daegu in 2002 to conduct research, explore new sources of financing, and integrate solar into local and national policy, and in 2004 Daegu enacted an Energy Code with the goal of "improving energy efficiency and city involvement in energy policy."[7]

A number of cities aspire to the title of "solar city," utilizing a variety of strategies and taking a number of positive steps to advance solar power and renewable energy. These municipal efforts demonstrate the considerable role cities can play in forging a renewable energy path. In no small part, this is about a new way of understanding cities. Renewable energy production can and should occur within cities, integrated into their land use and built form, and comprising a significant and important element of the urban economy. Cities are not simply consumers of energy, but catalysts for more sustainable energy paths. Cities can become part of the earth's solar cycle.

The shift in the direction to renewable cities can occur through many actions taken: demonstration solar or low energy homes created to show architects, developers, and citizens that green can be appealing (e.g., Chicago and Freiburg, Germany), procurement actions that source regionally produced wind and other renewable energy to power municipal lights and buildings (e.g., Santa Monica), and locally and regionally produced food for schools and other public venues (e.g., San Francisco is moving in this direction); green building standards, which at the highest level require renewable energy, for all new public as well as private buildings (many cities such as Seattle and Chicago now mandate minimum Leadership in Energy and Environmental Design (LEED) green building certification for new public structures; some cities like New York have adopted higher performance building standards in order to reach renewable energy targets. Over one hundred U.S. cities and towns have green building requirements for public projects, and a handful have adopted the principles for private projects. For example, Los Angeles now requires all private buildings over fifty thousand square feet to meet LEED standards,[8] and San Francisco is taking steps to require that all new large commercial buildings and residential high rises will include solar power, nontoxic paints, and water-saving fixtures.[9]

Many green building initiatives have already been mentioned, and this is where the greatest movement toward an urban renewable energy future has occurred. At the building level it is easier to integrate the necessary technology into new construction, and design improvements are an easier sell as the cost benefits are proven. Cleaner energy sources also minimize the carbon footprint of buildings. We discuss green building in more detail in the next section on the carbon neutral city.

Cities can underwrite the solar energy and renewable energy sectors, as Chicago has done. Barcelona has installed photovoltaic (PV) systems on the rooftops of two of the main buildings of its city hall, and the Australian cities of Adelaide and Melbourne have designated solar precincts where similar solar installations are being undertaken on civic buildings. Melbourne's CH2 building is a model as it exports renewable energy. The Australian government has a Solar Cities Program that funds demonstration solar regions in cities across the country. By offering incentives and/or mandating the use of renewable energy, cities can directly contribute to the economic viability of renewable energy technologies (reducing the cost of PVs, for instance), stimulate further private investment, and raise the public visibility of energy issues and opportunities. Simply allowing a consumer to see how much he or she is consuming and providing supply choices can result in increased support for renewables and in energy conservation. For example, Boulder, Colorado, is investing in a "smart grid," which uses broadband technology to better monitor use of energy throughout the city and gives consumers choices that allow them to be more energy efficient and choose the source of their power (wind, solar, or coal).[10] In Perth the Living Smart program gives people the chance for an eco-coach to come to their house and provide an audit of their energy, water, waste, and travel, and suggest options for them; many are choosing to add PVs when they learn that they will earn back the investment in less than a decade. Average greenhouse savings of around 1.5 tonnes per household are being achieved.[11]

Few cities have been as active in seeking and nurturing a reputation as a renewable city as Freiburg, Germany. Known to many as the "ecological capital of Europe" Freiburg has adopted an impressive and wide-ranging set of environmental planning and sustainability initiatives, many focused on renewable energy. Through its SolarRegion Freiburg program, the city has actively supported solar energy as an important element of its economic base, including the promotion of it as a form of local tourism. A series of "solar tours" have been organized, for instance, as a way to view and learn about the innovative solar energy projects in the city. And there are many such projects, from dramatic individual residences (e.g., Rolf Disch's Heliotropic House) to prototype experimental homes (e.g., the Freiburg zero-energy house) to business structures (e.g., the zero-emission Solar Fabrik, the Solar Tower, high-rise office building), and public buildings and installations. The city has also become home to an impressive number of scientific and educational organizations, including the Fraunhaufer Solar Institute and the

International Society for Solar Energy (ISES), among others. Freiburg has supported these organizations in different ways including offering ISES subsidized rent for the historic, city-owned structure that became its headquarters. Freiburg is one of the few cities that has recognized that the attraction of Sixth Wave businesses and expertise will give them an economic edge.

Freiburg has, moreover, incorporated renewable energy in all major new development areas, including Resielfeld and Vauban, which are new, compact, green areas, in the city that employ both active and passive solar techniques. The city also mandates a fairly stringent energy standard for all new homes. In Vauban, all the homes are very low-energy, many incorporating solar panels. Vauban also boasts an area of "plus-energy" homes that produce more power than they actually need, as well as solar office complex and two solar parking garages. The combined heat and power plant for Vauban uses waste wood.

The Victoria Hotel in the center of Freiburg now markets itself as the world's first zero-emission hotel, boasting that all its energy needs are satisfied through renewable energy sources, including solar. A host of other environmental features are available to guests, including free transit passes for riding the city's exemplary public transit system.

There are also impressive examples in the United States of cities promoting and supporting (some through financial incentives) the installation of solar and renewable energy technology. Austin, Texas, for instance, has set a target of fifteen megawatts of solar energy production by 2007, and has provided relatively generous rebates through its city-owned energy company (in 2007 at the rate of $4 per kilowatt; $4.50 for nonprofit organizations) for the installation of rooftop PV systems. These subsidies will typically cover between 45 percent and 75 percent of the cost of installing a rooftop PV system. Low-interest loans and rebates are offered for the installation of solar hot water heating systems.

San Francisco and Chicago have both installed PV systems on the rooftops of public structures (most notably on the Moscone Center in the case of San Francisco, and the Center for Green Technology in Chicago). The Moscone Center solar panels were funded through a voter-approved initiative and in partnership with the San Francisco Public Utilities Commission. The solar electrical system is capable of producing enough power for 550 homes annually. The Chicago Center for Green Technology has a LEED Platinum rating. As part of the project's water management system, a solar-powered fountain uses rainwater collected from the roof of the building. In Sacramento, California, new PV systems are being placed on car-parking structures, nature center rooftops, and recently on a structure in the Sacramento Zoo. Through the "Community Solar" program of the city's own utility district (SMUD), customers contribute to these installations through a modest rate premium (one cent per kilowatt hour above current rates). These cities have also taken many steps to reduce energy consumption in public buildings and facilities (e.g., conversion of traffic lighting to LED lights, lighting upgrades in public buildings).[12]

The city of Adelaide also envisions itself as a solar city, as a part of its larger green city initiative. Spearheaded by the Adelaide Capital City Committee, these efforts have already resulted in a Carbon Neutral Strategy and a number of solar projects, including the designation of the North Terrace Solar Precinct, and the installation of PVs on the rooftops of four government buildings: the South Australian Museum, Art Gallery, State Library, and Parliament House. The city's solar initiative was first funded by a federal grant from the Solar Cities Program. The city and state have been collaborating on a solar schools initiative, with the goal of 250 solar schools (schools with rooftop installations, and that incorporate solar and renewable energy into their educational curricula). This idea has since been taken up by the new Australian federal government to be applied to every school in the country. And most creatively the city has been installing grid-connected PV street lamps that produce some six times the energy needed for the lighting. These new lights are designed in a distinctive shape of a mallee tree, a eucalyptus tree native to the area, and are referred to as "solar mallees." This is one of the few examples of solar art or solar "place" projects.

Along with incentives (financial and otherwise), renewable cities recognize the need to set minimum regulatory standards. Barcelona has a solar ordinance that requires new buildings and substantial retrofits of existing buildings to obtain a minimum of 60 percent of hot water needs from solar. This has already led to a significant growth in that city in the number of solar thermal installations.

Sydney, Australia, in the state of New South Wales, has mandated that new homes must now be designed to produce 40 percent fewer greenhouse gas emissions than a standard house (after initially requiring 20 percent and finding it was relatively easy to achieve). They are also required to use 40 percent less water.

Chicago Center for Green Technology showing rooftop solar and Chicago skyline. (Credit: Timothy Beatley)

Carbon Neutral City: Every home, neighborhood, and business is carbon neutral.

In 2007 the head of News Corporation, Rupert Murdoch, the CEO of one of the biggest media empires in the world, announced that his company would be going carbon neutral. This has led to some remarkable innovation in the company as they confront the totally new territory of becoming a global leader in energy efficiency, renewable energy, and carbon offsets.

Many businesses, universities, and households are committing to minimizing their carbon footprint and even becoming carbon neutral. (Prince Charles has declared that his household and his charity organizations are carbon neutral.) But can it become a feature of whole neighborhoods and even complete cities?

Becoming carbon neutral for urban development will require a three-step process:

- reducing energy use wherever possible — especially in the building and transportation sectors;

- using renewable energy sources whenever possible, while being careful that the production of the renewable energy sources is not contributing significantly to greenhouse gases; and
- offsetting any CO_2 emitted through purchasing carbon credits, tree planting, or other renewable options.

Private initiatives focused on helping cities reach these goals include ICLEI's Cities for Climate Change, Architecture 2030, and The Clinton Foundation's C-40 Climate Change Initiative. As mentioned above, many municipalities have started to offer incentives and/or require that new buildings meet certain green-building standards. Minimizing carbon at the building level has momentum as it is easier to integrate the technology into new building, and the cost benefits have been proven (not just in energy savings, but in increased productivity and fewer sick days in green office buildings).[13]

By building green and retrofitting existing buildings to be more efficient, North American greenhouse gas emissions could be cut by 20 percent. As *Scientific American* reported in their 2007 article, "Green Buildings May Be Cheapest Way to Slow Global Warming," "North American homes, offices and other buildings contribute an estimated 2.2 billion tons of carbon dioxide to the atmosphere every year—more than one third of the continent's greenhouse gas pollution output."[14]

Details about global green building standards go beyond the scope of this book. But it is worth providing further information about the New South Wales BASIX approvals system (www.basix.nsw.gov.au). Its genius lies in being Web-based so it does not add to the huge amount of paperwork that has grown around most planning and design decisions. It is also flexible and can be adjusted for different climatic and soil zones. Owners wishing to build must achieve their BASIX certificate by choosing the best combinations of technologies, materials, and designs that suit them. After two years of operation the housing market has changed; gone are the black-roofed, no eaves or verandahs, poorly oriented houses with big air conditioners.

BASIX is calculated to have saved 8 million tons of CO_2 and 287 billion liters of water in ten years. The system has been extended to all new additions and alterations but not fully yet to high rise buildings, which is a pity.[15]

Similar to the BREEAM green building standards introduced in the United Kingdom in the 1990s, the U.S. Green Building Council

(USGBC) has created a very successful voluntary system to measure the energy saving and environmental "value" of a commercial and residential building, home, school, retail structure, interior, or neighborhood development (in pilot phase). While the U.S. system, known as Leadership in Energy and Environmental Design (LEED) has been criticized for its lack of geographic flexibility and minimal incentives to revitalize existing areas, among other things, it has been invaluable in setting a standard by which green buildings can be measured. A Canadian-based rating system, Green Globes, is designed to be simple and straightforward, and has been adopted by some U.S. communities and states (www.green globes.com).

Zero-energy buildings and homes go well beyond what is required by any green building rating system. These have been built in the Netherlands, Denmark, and Germany for at least ten years, and now increasingly positive examples are in every region of the world, including North America. In 2006 a Zero-Energy community opened in Sacramento. It is anticipated that residents of this community will spend up to 70 percent less on utilities than those living in comparable homes powered by conventional means.[16]

A major difference between the United States and Europe is that European government is generally more involved in requiring green building standards. Basic green building standards exist for the European Union (EU), and individual countries have their own requirements. For example, Germany requires that every worker must be within ten feet of natural daylight.

Many solar buildings in Australia, such as the Lend Lease building (30 The Bond), find that it is the way to attract the best and brightest graduates. The CH2 Melbourne City Council building cost over $50 million with some $12 million extra costs for its energy, water, and waste innovations (that gave it a six-star rating equivalent to LEED Platinum). The payback was going to be fifteen to twenty years but a study evaluating productivity gains found that over 10 percent increases had been found, which reduces the time for payback to less than ten years.[17]

The Macquarie Bank in Sydney decided to build a green building for their new headquarters in part due to the pressure from younger staff. The building is now to be the first six-star commercial building in Sydney and indicates that even in the banking industry a community-based design process can lead to the kind of resource productivity that we need for the future in our cities.[18]

Green buildings provide the basis for carbon neutral cities. (top) CH2 building for Melbourne City Council (Credit: City of Melbourne); (bottom) Solara in San Diego (Credit: Timothy Beatley)

BedZED in London, the first carbon neutral development in the UK. (Credit: Timothy Beatley)

While many mayors have committed to reducing their carbon footprint, it is a complicated task to implement policy that will reduce carbon beyond the single-building level. But again, there are hopeful examples. One is BedZED—or Beddington Zero Energy Development—the first carbon neutral eco-community in the United Kingdom. Here, a new neighborhood of green flats and live-work units in the London borough of Sutton demonstrates a new kind of "solar urbanism"—it is also next to a train station. This is not an agenda of sacrifice at all, and once one sees the flats awash in sunlight, the unusual rooftop gardens (sky gardens), and the other impressive elements of this neighborhood such as its social housing arrangements, one imagines that sustainable living would be a relatively easy sell; comfort and a high quality of life are maximized, not sacrificed, through such a zero-energy, carbon neutral vision. Estimates suggest that residents are able to reduce their ecological footprints by a third (and live with a footprint less than half of that of an American) simply by moving into BedZED.

The UK government has, since BedZED was built in 2002, mandated that all urban development will be carbon neutral by 2016 with a phasing in beginning in 2009. The mayor of London has requested that each of his thirty-two boroughs set up demonstration carbon neutral developments in 2007 and 2008, many of which are underway. Each local government in the UK needs to produce a Carbon Neutral Strategy to show how they are going to create a carbon-reduced future.

Malmö, Sweden, has stated that it has already become a carbon neutral city; Växjä, Sweden, has declared its intention to become a fossil-fuel-free city, and Newcastle, United Kingdom, and Adelaide, Australia, aspire to be carbon neutral. Each has taken important steps in the direction of renewable energy consistent with the "renewable city vision" articulated here. In all Australian cities, the carbon and GHG emissions associated with many municipal motor pools are being offset through innovative tree-planting initiatives and organizations like GreenFleet, which has recently planted its two-millionth tree. Transportation companies such as airlines offer a carbon neutral service, schools like South Fremantle High School and many businesses like News Corporation are committed to being carbon neutral. The carbon offsetting is accredited through a federal government scheme called Greenhouse Friendly and provides a strong legal backing to ensure that plantations are real, are related to the money committed, and are guaranteed for at least seventy years as required by the Kyoto Convention. Many of the funds from the carbon offsetting programs are going to biodiversity plantations that are regenerating the bioregional ecology around the cities (e.g., Gondwana Link).

In addition to helping to sequester carbon, trees help to naturally cool buildings and homes and can reduce the need to use energy necessary for artificial cooling. Initiatives to provide greater tree coverage include the tree planting program at the Sacramento Municipal Utility District (SMUD). SMUD has been actively promoting tree planting as a way of reducing energy consumption and addressing the urban heat island problem. Since 1990, this program, which provides residents with free shade trees, has resulted in the planting of some 350,000 trees (www.smud.org). This program could be expanded to provide residents and businesses with carbon neutral options.

As part of Atlanta's ambitious beltline project to connect trails, transit, greenspace, and development along twenty-two miles of an old rail corridor, over 1,200 acres of new greenspace will be added to the urban landscape. And in Los Angeles, Mayor Villaraigosa has committed to planting one million trees through the urban area, made possible by public–private partnerships.

At a national level, recognizing the value of trees to a community, the Home Depot Foundation has a major initiative to support the planting and care of urban trees. They believe that trees "are essential to a supportive healthy community."[19]

The next step is to commit to a comprehensive carbon neutral approach that can link their tree planting to a broader cause. In doing so, we can raise urban and bioregional reforestation to a new level and provide hope for citizens who are looking for ways to contribute to reducing the impact of climate change.[20]

Carbon neutral strategies are an important part of the policy agenda for local governments and city-regional governments, not only for lessening our impact on climate change, but for reducing our dependence on oil. They need to drive this part of the resilient city agenda.

In Europe and Australia carbon neutral city initiatives do not yet include transport. Regional carbon neutral strategies are needed for managing the transition to renewables so households and businesses are not simply adding on through the present distribution system. However, there are more fundamental things happening that are changing the way power is provided in cities.

Distributed City: Cities will shift from large centralized power, water, and waste systems to small-scale and neighborhood-based systems.

In global cities, especially in the United States and Australia, the belief seems to be that the most effective and efficient approach to providing energy is through large centralized production facilities and extensive distribution systems that transport energy relatively long distances. Most power systems for the past hundred years have become bigger and more centralized. Post-peak oil, low-carbon cities assume a more decentralized energy production system, using smaller-scale technologies, where production is more neighborhood-based and relatively small scale.

Whether a wind turbine, small biomass CHP plant, or a rooftop photovoltaic system, renewable energy is produced closer to where it is consumed, and indeed directly by those who consume it. This approach is often referred to as "distributed energy" or "distributed generation" and offers a number of benefits, including energy savings through the ability to better control power production, lower vulnerability, and greater resilience in the face of natural and human-caused disaster (including terrorist attacks). (The same idea is being used for water and waste.) Clever integration of these small power plants into a grid can be achieved with new control systems that balance demand and supply from a range of sources as they rise and fall. Small-scale energy systems are an essential part of the resilient city of the future.

In June 2008 Perth's natural gas supply was interrupted by a massive explosion in a gas facility, cutting off forty percent of the gas supply for two months. Huge economic costs were carried by industries that had to close and others who had to buy expensive diesel as a replacement fuel for their industrial heat. The vulnerability of the city was exposed. If Perth had moved to distributed power and heat systems it would have been much more resilient.

The cost of providing the infrastructure necessary for distributed power, water, and waste systems is not a significant issue. For example, in Hopetoun, a remote settlement in Western Australia, a mining company and the state government had to assess how best to build the town's infrastructure to support a large influx of people for a new mining venture. They assessed three options: centralized, distributed, and decentralized (household based). The results showed the distributed option was half the cost of the others and would save $0.5 billion. However, the utilities were not keen to do it as they were not familiar with the approach.[21]

While many sense that renewable energy techniques and technologies are potentially quite useful, others argue that they are for the most part not suited to urban settings, where significant numbers of people live and where development patterns may be quite dense. Part of the paradigm shift will involve refuting or moving beyond this aversion to urban settings as the sites for production. Large solar production projects, for instance, or wind energy farms, it is commonly thought, require relatively remote sites (in part to minimize perceived conflicts with residents and communities). But today there are photovoltaics on roof tops, micro turbine wind systems on roof ridges and edges to buildings, geothermal power and air conditioning from shallow hot water, and small wave power technologies that can feed directly into coastal cities. Integrating renewable energy sources into urban areas is not only necessary for resilience but makes energy, and solar energy in particular, a visible part of communities. There are many ways that small-scale solar projects can be incorporated into an urban area and there is an increasing number of good case studies showing the possibilities.

The city of Honolulu, for instance, under the leadership of former mayor Jeremy Harris, has been installing small wind turbines on parking lot light poles and many possibilities exist for micro-turbine or small wind turbine applications on rooftops. (Honolulu happens to be ranked first as the lowest carbon emitting city in the United States.[22])

The Dutch Pavilion at the Hannover World's Fair in 2000 demonstrated convincingly that even fairly large turbines (in this case especially designed by the company Largerwey) could function quite well on a five-story structure.

In North America, few metropolitan areas are making as much progress in harnessing solar energy as Toronto, spurred on by a combination of grassroots interest and activism and some new and impressive economic incentives. In 2006 a law passed that mandates all of Ontario province's ninety utilities must purchase renewable energy from small producers at premium prices. The law requires that utilities pay forty-two cents per kilowatt-hour for solar, making this the most generous form of production subsidy available in North America. Predating the Ontario law, neighborhoods in Toronto had been organizing and forming buying cooperatives, in which they pooled their buying power to negotiate special reduced prices from local PV companies. It all began in the east end, where residents of the Riverdale neighborhood formed the first of these solar buying clubs. A new neighborhood organization was created—the Riverdale Initiative for Solar Energy, or RISE—and eventually about seventy-five residents joined together to purchase rooftop PV systems, resulting in about a 15 percent savings in their purchase cost. The Toronto (and Ontario province) example suggests the merits of combining bottom-up neighborhood solar activism with top-down incentives and encouragement. As other neighborhoods embrace solar energy Toronto will likely emerge as a successful model of how to stimulate the transition to a distributed city.

In Europe support for small-scale production—offered through what are commonly referred to as Standard Offer Contracts (SOCs, often known as "feed in tariffs")—has been extremely successful. In Germany, solar production is reportedly now growing by 35 to 50 percent per year, in response to these incentives, already resulting in a hundred thousand grid-connected PV systems (and two gigawatts of solar production). At this rate of growth, all energy in Germany, by some estimates, could come from clean and renewable sources by as early as 2040. All of this came from a bottom-up campaign, which culminated in the impressive 2001 German Renewable Energy Sources Act. This shows how rapidly a country can address the solar city agenda once the bottom-up processes are translated into a powerful piece of legislation, which provides ordinary householders with the means to join the solar distributed city.

One very positive model can be seen in the redevelopment of the Western Harbor in Malmö, Sweden. Here the goal was to achieve 100 percent renewable energy, produced from local sources. This has been realized by incorporating into the fabric of this new urban neighborhood a mix of renewable energy production ideas and technologies, including a wind turbine and facade-mounted solar hot water collectors. The solar panels are a visible feature of this delightful urban district, which boasts other sustainability initiatives (innovative storm water management, habitat and biotope restoration, and green courtyards and green rooftops).[23]

In Kronsberg, an ecological urban district in the German city of Hannover, a number of low energy or renewable energy ideas have been integrated into this compact, walkable community. Three relatively large wind turbines (the largest a 1.8 megawatt turbine) have been sited just a few hundred meters from some residences, and many of the apartments are supplied by a centralized solar hot water heating system. District heating and two small combined heat and power stations (one in the basement of a residential building) provide the neighborhood's remaining hot water needs and produce electricity. The use of district heating, and combined heat and power plants, has become a standard design feature in new European developments and is a much more efficient and sustainable way to heat and power communities.[24]

Perth, Australia, has long been committed to using solar for hot water and home heating as it has six months of hot dry weather with an average of over three hundred cloudless days a year. Until the 1980s around 40 percent of homes had solar water heaters and the local industry exported them around the world. Perth homes were rarely air conditioned and few had central heating as they were designed to use the sun effectively. However in the 1980s natural gas was brought to the city as part of a major development scheme and was heavily subsidized to help the industry get established (this is the same gas pipeline that was cut by an explosion described earlier). Solar heaters started to give way to central air-conditioning and heating because it was so inexpensive. Houses became poorly designed with little relation to their solar context. Peak power problems developed on hot summer days and now the government needs to try to reduce the air conditioning load. It has also been discovered that shallow, warm groundwater can be tapped and passed through a heat exchanger to enable buildings to be heated and cooled from a local renewable source. Thus, Perth has the opportunity to tap a distributed renewable energy source, along with its older solar heating and building orientation, to replace a considerable part of its natural gas and electricity load. The opportunity to do so after their vulnerability was exposed is perhaps not the best way to make this transition.

Despite these growing examples of how small-scale systems can be integrated into an urban grid, there are no obvious examples yet of a management system that incorporates local systems and their users in a decentralized, distributed model (although initiatives such as the smart grid technology under development in Boulder will allow homes with solar energy to plug into the grid).

Perhaps Vauban is the best available model, especially as it was planned and built around a community-based model by Forum Vauban. This Public Community Partnership (PCP) model is how the switch to distributed systems is likely to be driven. The beginnings of such a model can be seen in a new urban-fringe development in Perth called The Vale. Although it began as a typical car-dependent suburban development, the developers, Multiplex, are trying to see how they can retrofit existing areas and determine how the next stages can be more sustainable. Groundwater in the area is easily contaminated as the development is on sand, which drains into some important wetlands and creeks. The local and state government has allowed the development only if it can create a mechanism for managing the drainage from the area so that it does not impact the wetlands. Residents are being instructed on how to manage their gardens and are being enlisted into a community association that can help to manage the wetlands and associated open space.

Homeowners, including those who have bought land and are about to begin building, are given help in designing and retrofitting their houses for solar gain, and creating gardens with native plantings and low water needs. Seminars and workshops are held on how to link into community services and local employment. On new streets, householders are being shown how to plant front yards so that a bush garden is created from one end of a street to another with a gradation in the native bushes designed so that birds and insects can find food somewhere along the street regardless of the season. Bicycle paths link the houses to schools, community centers, shops, and the main transit stop. All of these factors are helping to grow local social capital and create a stronger sense of place.

The community association could be the basis for managing a range of local infrastructure such as renewable power and even local water supply for gardens through community groundwater bores.

To move the implementation of distributed infrastructure beyond these few cities, utilities will need to develop models with city planners of how they can do local energy planning with community-based

The Vale in Perth has developed a community association for managing local sustainability issues such as community planting of front yards for biodiversity and water management. Can it grow into a model for managing decentralized technology in cities? (Credit Peter Newman)

approaches. They will need to coordinate with local management to ensure that the best features of renewable energy are integrated in a way that is coherent and technically acceptable. The same opportunities exist for water utilities, but the issues of peak oil and climate change should compel energy planners to more urgently adjust to this new localized planning agenda of the distributed city.

Photosynthetic City: The potential to harness renewable energy and provide food and fiber locally will become part of urban green infrastructure

There has been a positive trend in planning in the direction of an expanded notion of urban infrastructure to include the idea of "green infrastructure."[25] Green infrastructure refers to the many green and ecological features and systems, from wetlands to urban forests, that provide a host of benefits to cities and urban residents—clean water, storm water collection and management, climate moderation, and cleansing of urban air, among others. Yet, this understanding of green infrastructure as part of the working landscape of cities and metropolitan areas does not yet extend to include the sources of renewable energy, or local food and fiber, as potential green infrastructure. We are referring to this expanded definition of green infrastructure as "photosynthetic" infrastructure.

In addition to the potential to tap the sun, wind, and heat of the earth (geothermal) for renewable energy, the use of crops (as shown by the bio-fuel industry) and wood shows·promise for small-scale, decentralized use. The transition to growing fuels will need to be tailored to new crops and forests that can feed into new ways of fueling our buildings and vehicles. Especially promising is the notion of viewing farms and landscapes, open areas in and around cities, as potential sources of renewable energy, especially the production of biocrops and biofuels. The link between city and hinterland can be built into a closer relationship in the resilient city of the future. This will mean more intensive greening of the lower-density parts of a city and its peri-urban regions with renewable energy crops and forests, while continuing to see how centers and corridors can be developed at higher density for better transit and walkability. Growing crops for fuel in urban areas must be balanced with the need to grow food locally in these areas. Ideally fuel would be generated from byproducts of these efforts.

The city of Växjä in Sweden has developed a locally based renewable energy strategy that takes full advantage of its working landscapes, in its case the abundant forests that exist within close proximity of the city. Växjä's main power plant, formerly fueled by oil, has been converted to biomass, almost entirely now from wood chips, most of which are a byproduct of commercial logging in the region. The wood, more specifically, comes from the branches, bark, and tops of trees, and is derived from within one hundred kilometers of the power plant. This combined heat and power plant (Sandvik II) provides all the town's heating needs and much of its electricity needs, and its conversion to biomass as a fuel has been a key element in the city's aspiration to become an oil-free city. Each city must develop its own mix of local renewable sources but Växjä has demonstrated that it can transition from an oil-based power system to a completely renewable system without losing its economic edge. Indeed cities that develop such resiliency early are likely to have an edge as oil and gas resources decline.

The Vauban eco-village in Freiburg, Germany, has a cogeneration power plant using wood chips generated from local forestry. The plant provides the five thousand residents and one thousand local businesses with heat and power. Vauban's buildings also contain some 450 square meters of solar water heating panels and 1,200 square meters of PV collectors.

The metropolitan landscape can be viewed as the pallet for a creative mix of solar design and renewable energy projects, and every city and region will have its own special opportunities and local resources. Copenhagen demonstrates the possibility of integrating wind into the urban form of a place through its Middelgrunden wind farm. Consisting of twenty-two-megawatt wind turbines, located just offshore of the city's harbor, they blend in harmoniously with the contours and surroundings of this urbanized coast. The subject of extensive visual impact studies, the turbines provide energy sufficient for about thirty-five thousand residents of this region.

San Francisco has been actively exploring both tidal and wave energy, both in abundance in this coastal city. There are many other examples from which to learn, but it is important to search out the unique opportunities that exist in each city and metro area with the view that developing the renewable energy infrastructure of a place is just as important as the other more conventional forms of infrastructure such as water supply, sewer, and waste disposal. One of the most important potential biofuel sources of the future will be blue-green algae that can be grown intensively on roof tops. Blue-green algae can photosynthesize so requires only sun, water, and nutrients. The output from blue-green algae is ten times faster than most other biomass sources so it can be continuously cropped and fed into a process for producing biofuels or small-scale electricity. Most importantly city buildings can all utilize their roofs to tap solar energy and use it for local purposes without the distribution or transport losses so apparent in our cities today. Bill McDonough says that "every roof should be photosynthetic"; by this he means either green roofs for biodiversity/ water collection/landscaping, PV collectors, or biofuel algal collectors. This can become a policy mandated by local governments.[26]

Municipal comprehensive plans typically inventory and describe a host of natural and economic resources found within the boundaries of a city—from mineral sites to historic buildings to biodiversity—but estimating incoming renewable energy (sun, wind, wave, biomass, or geothermal) is usually not included. But in advancing the renewable energy agenda in Barcelona, the city did take the step of calculating incoming solar gain. As former sustainable city councilor Josep Puig notes, this amounts to "10 times more than the energy the city consumes or 28 times more than the electricity the city is consuming." The issue now is how to tap into this across the city.[27]

The first step for any city is to see its potential renewable sources. Partly this is about looking at the urban environment in new ways. A school is not just a school, a library not just a library, a parking garage not just a parking garage, but they are potential power-generating plants as well. In some ways this is a natural extension of the shift in urban planning toward a multiple-use, mixed-use view of cities and regions (integrating power production in a vertical as well as a horizontal mix). Also, this suggests an agenda of shifting the way we see and appreciate the benefits that flow from a building project or facility. The potential for long-term cost savings, and many other kinds of benefits, from designing say a solar school, extend well beyond the typical or conventional cost–benefit calculation process.

As well as renewable fuel, cities must also incorporate food in this more holistic solar and post-oil view for the future. Food, in the globalized marketplace, increasingly travels great distances—apples from New Zealand, grapes from Chile, wine from South Australia. Food miles are rising, and already food in the United States travels a distance of between 1,500 to 2,500 miles from where it is grown to where it is consumed. These exotic sources of food come at a high energy cost. Thomas Starrs cleverly refers to modern food as "The SUV in Our Pantry," in an article in *Solar Today* magazine:

> It takes about 10 fossil fuel calories to produce each food calorie in the average American diet. So if your daily food intake is 2,000 calories, then it took about 20,000 calories to grow that food and get it to you. In more familiar units, this means that growing, processing and delivering the food consumed by a family of four each year requires the equivalent of almost 34,000 kilowatt-hours of energy, or more than 930 gallons of gasoline. (For comparison, the average U.S. household annually consumes about 10,800 kilowatt-hours of electricity, or about 1,070 gallons of gasoline.) In other words, we use about as much energy to grow our food as to power our homes or fuel our cars.[28]

We have good examples of urban (and suburban) communities that design in or create spaces for community gardens, urban farms, and edible landscapes and attempt to satisfy a considerable portion of food needs on-site or nearby. It is possible to trade hardscape environments for fruit trees and edible perennials, as shown by a project in the downtown

Vancouver neighborhood of Mole Hill. Here a conventional alleyway has been converted to a green and luxurious network of edible plants and raised-bed gardens to create an inviting, pedestrianized community space, where the occasional automobile now seems out of place. New urban development can and should include places (rooftops, sideyards, backyards) where residents can grow food. This has been a trend in Europe, as new urban ecological neighborhoods include community gardens as a central design element (e.g., Viikki, in Helsinki, South False Creek in Vancouver). Integrating new development and food production is also happening in some innovative ways in the United States. One very good example comes from Madison, Wisconsin, where a project called Troy Gardens has emerged from excess land owned by a state-owned mental hospital. Called the accidental eco-village by those involved in its transformation, the land was being sold in 1995 when the community members who had been using it as a garden and park stepped in and formed an association to buy the land. Through partnerships with other NGOs and the University of Wisconsin–Madison Department of Urban and Regional Planning, the Friends of Troy Gardens was able to create a diversity of uses to finance the purchase of the land. The site is now a mixed-income co-housing project with thirty housing units, a community garden with 320 allotments, an intensive urban farm using traditional Hmong agricultural techniques for a community supported agricultural enterprise, and a prairie restoration scheme that is regenerating local biodiversity.[29]

Cities need to find creative ways to promote urban farming where it is feasible and not in tension with the need to redevelop for reduced car dependence. This may mean that a city can utilize the many vacant lots for commercial and community farms in areas that have been blighted (e.g., the estimated seventy thousand vacant lots in Chicago alone). However if these areas are well served with good transit and other infrastructure then such uses should be seen as temporary and indeed can be part of the rehabilitation of an area leading to the redevelopment of eco-villages that are car free and models of solar building. Many cities have embarked on some form of effort to examine community food security and to promote more sustainable local and regional food production. These can be integrated into ecologically sustainable urban rehabilitation projects.[30]

Localizing much of the production of fiber and building materials provides tremendous new opportunities to build more sustainable place-economies. Dramatic reductions in the energy consumed by transport-

Troy Gardens in Madison, Wisconsin, combines a commercial farm, community garden (above), prairie restoration, and a cohousing development. (Credit: Timothy Beatley)

ing these materials is, of course, the primary benefit, but local economies can also become more resilient in the face of global economic forces. It is also about reforming lost connections to place, to sustaining land-scapes, and ultimately to human relationships and (at least partially) over-coming the stifling anonymity that characterizes our age.

At the BedZED project in London, more than half of the building materials for the project came from within a thirty-five-mile radius, and the wood used in construction, as well as for fuel in the neighborhood's CHP plant, derives from local council forests. City dwellers are already asking where their food is grown, where wine comes from, where the ma-terials that make up their furniture come from. This understanding can help to support not just a slow-food movement for local foods, but a slow-fiber and slow-materials movement for local fabric and building purposes.

Eco-Efficient City: Cities and regions will move from linear to circular or closed-loop systems, where substantial amounts of their energy and material needs are provided from waste streams

A more integrated notion of energy entails seeing cities as complex meta-bolic systems (not unlike a human body) with flows and cycles and where, ideally, the things that have traditionally been viewed as negative outputs (e.g., solid waste, wastewater) are re-envisioned as productive inputs to satisfy other urban needs, including energy. The sustainability movement has long been advocating for a shift away from the current view of cities as linear resource-extracting machines. This is often described as the eco-efficiency agenda.[31]

The eco-efficiency agenda has been taken up by the United Nations and the World Business Council on Sustainable Development, with an ambitious target for industrialized countries of a tenfold reduction in consumption of resources by 2040, along with rapid transfers of knowledge and technology to developing countries. While this eco-efficiency agenda is a huge challenge, it is important to remember that throughout the Industrial Revolution of the past two hundred years, human productivity has increased by 20,000 percent. The Sixth Wave has the potential to create the kind of eco-efficiency gains that are required.[32]

The eco-efficient city agenda includes William McDonough's "cradle to cradle" concept for the design of all new products, and ideas from industrial ecology where industries share resources and wastes like an ecosystem. Good examples exist in Kalundborg, Germany, and Kwinana, Australia.[33]

The view of cities as a complex set of metabolic flows might also help guide us in dealing with those situations (especially in the shorter term) where some degree of reliance on resources and energy from other regions and parts of the world still occurs. Understanding that food transported to large American cities, despite great efforts to promote local and regional production, will still occur, suggests that efforts should be made to mitigate or compensate for the energy consumed and carbon emitted in this process. Perhaps that means contributions to a fund by which solar and renewable energy projects are supported in these regions and countries, or carbon sequestration projects. This view of cities suggests the need to forge new sustainable (and equitable) relationships between and among regions in the world, where cities strive for a new sustainable relationship with their rural *and* international hinterlands. Examples include sustainable sourcing agreements, region-to-region trade agreements, and urban procurement systems based on green certification systems, among others. Embracing a metabolic view of cities and metropolitan areas takes us in some interesting and useful directions.

This new paradigm of sustainable urban metabolism will require profound changes in the way we conceptualize cities and metropolitan regions as well as in the ways we plan and manage them. New forms of cooperation and collaboration between municipal agencies, various urban actors, and stakeholder groups will be required; for instance, municipal departments will need to formulate and implement integrated resource flows strategies. New organizational and governance structures will likely be necessary as well as new planning tools and methods, which will, for example, allow us to map the resource flows of a city and region, will become standard in preparing comprehensive plans.

An example of this is Toronto's trash-to-can program, which allows the city to capture methane from waste to generate electricity. This not only reuses waste and provides an inexpensive energy source, but captures a significant amount of methane that would otherwise be released in the air. (Before it reached capacity in its operation, it is estimated that the Keele Valley Landfill generated $3 to $4 million annually, and provided enough power for approximately twenty-four thousand homes.[34])

One powerful example of how this "metabolic-flows" view can manifest in a new approach to urban design and building can be seen in the new dense urban neighborhood of Hammarby Sjöstad, in Stockholm. Here, from the beginning of the planning for this new district, an effort was made to think holistically, to understand the inputs, outputs, and resources that would be required and that would result. For instance, about a thousand apartments in Hammarby Sjöstad are equipped with stoves run on biogas extracted from wastewater generated in the community. Biogas also provides fuel for buses that serve the area. Organic waste from the community is returned to the neighborhood in the form of district heating and cooling. Some of the many other important design features include the close proximity of the community to central Stockholm and the installation of a high-frequency light rail system that makes it possible to live without a private automobile (there are also thirty vehicles in the neighborhood available for car-sharing). While not a perfect example, it represents a new and valuable way to see cities, and requires a degree of interdisciplinary and intersectoral collaboration that is still rare in most cities.

Place-Based City: Cities and regions will understand renewable energy more generally as a way to build local economy, nurture a high quality of life, and create a strong commitment to place

Local economic development has many advantages for the triple bottom line, including the creation of more local jobs, which greatly lessens the

Hammarby Sjöstad a new kind of eco-efficient city. (Credit: Timothy Beatley)

impact of commuting. Finding ways to help facilitate local enterprises becomes a major achievement in moving toward a less oil-constrained community. Michael Shuman has pioneered efforts to help small towns in the United States to grow their own jobs. Internationally Ernesto Sirolli has developed an approach to creating local enterprises that builds on the passions and resources of the local community and supports local businesses in their early vulnerable steps. The inaugural Enterprise Facilitation project to create local jobs was pioneered in Esperance, Western Australia, in 1985 but has since spread across three continents. Chair of the Esperance Project, Barrie Stearne, says: "We are proud to say almost 800 businesses—or 60 percent of the entrepreneurs we met—are still running successful, sustainable operations and have contributed more than $190 million in revenue to the local economy." What Sirolli and Shuman have both found time and time again is that place really matters. When people belong and have an identity in their town or city they want to put down their roots and create local enterprise.[35]

The first priority of most city officials is local economic development. They often fail to recognize that the best approach is to emphasize their local place identity, and very few relate this to solar energy as an economic resource to be tapped. Energy expenditures—by municipalities, companies, and individuals—represent a significant economic drain, as the energy often goes far beyond the community and region. Producing power from solar, wind, or biomass in the locality or region has the power to generate local jobs and economic revenue for lands and landscapes (farmland) that might otherwise be economically marginal, and recirculate dollars with an important economic multiplier effect.

Research on renewable energy and the creation of related products have developed into strong parts of the economy in Freiburg, Germany. According to city figures, the installation of solar panels and purifying wastewater account for 3 percent of jobs in the region.[36]

Moving toward the resilient city can also be seen as a local community development exercise. All the efforts at localizing energy, food, materials, and economic development remain dependent on the strength of local community. BedZed shows the critical importance of thinking beyond the design of the buildings themselves and seeing urban development through a more holistic community-oriented design lens. However impressive the passive solar design and smaller energy demands of this project are (three hundred millimeter insulation and an innovative ventilation and heat recovery system, for instance) much of the sustainable gain will come from how residents actually live in these places. Here, residents are being challenged to rethink their consumption and mobility decisions—there is a car-sharing club on site, for example, a food buying club, and the emergence of a community of residents helping each to think about and creatively reduce their ecological footprints. This is a hallmark of European green projects and an important lesson seen in other projects.

When Jan Scheurer examined a range of European urban ecology innovations, he found that when the innovations came from a close and committed community they were much more likely to stick and become ingrained into the lifestyles of the residents, giving the next generation a real opportunity to gain from them. However, many architect-designed innovations that were imposed on residents without their involvement or education of their value and use tended to fall into neglect or were actively removed. The resilient city requires that we pay closer attention to people and community development in the process of change. This localized approach will be critical to the peak oil transition. It creates the necessary innovation as people dialogue about the options to be oil-free, which in turn creates social capital as the basis for on-going community life and economic development.[37]

Above, numerous reasons have been presented for why a more localized approach will save oil, minimize greenhouse gas emissions, and help create better local economies and communities. Underneath the desire to develop more local personal relationships (as shown in projects like BedZED and Vauban) is the desire to belong to and be identified with a place.[38]

Sustainable Transport City: Cities, neighborhoods, and regions will be designed to use energy sparingly by offering walkable, transit-oriented options for all, supplemented by electric vehicles.

Given the importance of transportation in shaping and transitioning to resilient cities, the entire next chapter is devoted to it.

The agenda for future resilient cities is to have sustainable options available so that a city can indeed reduce its driving or VMT (vehicle miles traveled) 25 to 50 percent by 2050.

The denser a city the less its residents drive, the more they use transit, walk, and bike. This suggests that people drive mostly because they have no other alternative. Providing density to support transit, walking, and biking is a critical component to lessening oil dependence and reducing greenhouse gas emissions. In the United States, according to a 2007 study, "shifting 60 percent of new growth to compact patterns would save 85 million metric tons of CO_2 annually by 2030."[39]

While major cities such as New York and Chicago are dense and walkable, and their mayors have been lauded for their green plans and for signing onto the Mayor's Climate Change Initiative, the mass transit systems for these cities continue to experience budget cuts. The city of Seattle, whose mayor is credited with initiating the Mayor's Climate Change Initiative, has struggled to implement a rail system. And while the state of California is a global leader on some state initiatives it has not yet developed a plan for how its heavily oil-dependent cities will wean themselves off their tarry fix nor has the governor supported the popular fast rail initiative between San Francisco and Los Angeles. It is not the time for American cities to be complacent about oil.

While greening buildings, looking to renewable fuel sources, and creating more walkable communities are critical pieces of resiliency, investing in viable, accessible transit systems for our major metropolitan areas is the most important component for cities to become resilient in the face of waning oil sources and to minimize the impact of urban areas on climate change. As will be shown in the next chapter, transit not only saves oil, it also helps restructure a city so that it can begin the exponential reduction in oil so necessary for the future.

Conclusions

Resilience requires communities to be real and adaptable to whatever threat comes along. When people live in fear they do not join civil society groups as Robert Putnam found when examining the differences between the north and south of Italy. People in civil society groups are able to respond to all kinds of innovations and issues in their communities through the social capital that they have developed, through networks of trust and hope. Putnam found that this was the basis of vital economic development as well as sound environmental management.[40]

Thus resilient cities will have strong social capital, which will strengthen their ability to respond to the challenge of rethinking how their city is powered, where and how their resources originate, and how they travel. These issues of change in how we manage our cities and how we refuel them are fundamental to how we address peak oil and climate change. Change is not primarily about technology, but about how cities function at a basic cultural level. The necessary technologies will be adopted if we are able to create strong communities of hope that will take on these issues with confidence and strong political commitment.

5

Hope for Resilient Cities: Transport

The Oil Drum, a major peak oil Web site, predicted that we will not only pay a hundred dollars a barrel for oil but "$100 for a tank of gas." This prediction was made in 2006, long before oil hit a record $138 a barrel in 2008. While high prices have stirred mild panic in some, Matthew Simmons, founder of an energy investment banking firm, believes this is just the beginning and we will be faced with prices closer to three hundred dollars per barrel in the future.[1]

In a ranking of U.S. cities in their ability to cope with an oil crisis, New York was seen as the most prepared. New York uses just 326 gallons per person compared to Atlanta's 782 (the top of the unresilient list). There is a strong negative correlation between how much fuel a city uses and how much transit it has. In U.S. cities like Atlanta, San Diego, Denver, Houston, and Phoenix, transit accounts for less than 1 percent of motorized transportation; Washington, San Francisco, and Chicago are at 5 percent; and the best U.S. city, New York, has 9 percent.[2] Many of these cities are changing as they build new transit systems and extend existing service, but global comparisons show that U.S. cities are way behind most others in the world in level of transit ridership..

Australian, Canadian, and New Zealand cities are just a little better, varying from 5 percent in Perth (up to 10 percent in 2006), 7 percent in Vancouver, 12 percent in Sydney, and 14 percent in Toronto. Many European cities are over 20 percent transit (Zurich 24 percent, Munich 30 percent) with Barcelona and Rome at 35 percent. Although some European cities need to catch up, such as Glasgow, Marseille, and Geneva, which are all at 10 percent and Lyon at 8 percent, eastern European cities like Krakow are all around 50 percent transit.

The wealthy Asian cities are very high in transit (apart from the new Japanese city of Sapporo at 21 percent and Taipei at 25 percent) with

Singapore and Seoul at 40 percent, Tokyo and Osaka at around 60 percent, and Hong Kong at 73 percent.

Developing cities are highly variable, with Mumbai at the top with 84 percent transit; Dakar, Chennai, and Shanghai at around 70 percent; Beijing and Tunis at around 50 percent, Kuala Lumpur at 11 percent; Ho Chi Minh City at 8 percent; and Riyadh at 1 percent.

The compact nature of development and sound walking and biking infrastructure make it easier for European cities to average 34 percent walking or biking to work. Cities like Copenhagen, Paris, and Amsterdam have high bicycling rates that continue to increase due to the exceptional provision of support infrastructure in recent years.

Transportation already accounts for 15 percent of carbon emissions worldwide. In the United States it is predicted to be the largest growth in terms of CO_2 emissions (between 1996 and 2020). Approximately 28 percent of all energy used in America is consumed by transportation. This reflects a growth of 17 percent in transportation energy between 1995 and 2005 and the continuing descent of American cities into car dependence.[3]

There are many reasons—environmental, economic, health, and social—to overcome car dependence. They are best expressed now in terms of the lack of resilience, which combines all these factors. A city needs many kinds of transportation and land use options, not just one type, to be resilient. This choice is what Eric Britton, an American transport planner living in Paris, calls the New Mobility Agenda—breaking the stranglehold of the single "car-only" option for cities. This is not unlike Jane Jacobs's approach to making a city's economy more resilient through increasing the diversity of its economic functions or the approach of planning Professor Leonie Sandercock to increasing social resiliency through the acceptance of diversity. Brad Allenby and Jonathan Fink, academics at Arizona State University, discuss the inherent resiliency of communities based on a similar approach but add the important dimension of how the city is linked together through networks. These networks are what enable the city to respond to and be resilient in the face of disturbances. Put simply, if a city has an accessible, efficient, affordable transit system that can be expanded quickly to cope with increasing numbers, it will be much more resilient than one with a poor, largely inaccessible transit system that is quickly filled just as its highway system fills every day.[4]

As mentioned above, the global cities' data show that the New York urban region is the best U.S. city when it comes to per capita fuel use; however, Vancouver, Toronto, Perth, and Sydney consume approximately

A light rail links the ecological village of Vauban with downtown Freiburg, Germany. (Credit: Timothy Beatley)

half of the fuel of New York; and most European cities use only half of that. And New York (at 326 gallons per person) looks even less impressive when compared with Helsinki (at 69 gallons per person). In the wealthy Asian cities like Tokyo and Singapore fuel drops to a tenth of U.S. cities (Hong Kong uses 32 gallons per person). Chinese cities are almost off the scale in comparison with around 13 gallons of per capita fuel use. So while China is using a lot of oil for its intercity freight movements (that will now require a very large commitment to rail expansion) and it continues to build coal-fired power plants for its electricity, it is not anywhere close to the United States in overall rate of fuel consumption on a per capita basis.

So resiliency is relative. The New York urban region does have the best infrastructure and urban form to respond to declining oil dependence in the United States; indeed the city of New York uses just eighty gallons per person due to its density and transit base and over half of New Yorkers do not own a car; compared to only 8 percent of non–car owners nationally. But U.S. cities in general are out-consuming oil in similar Western cities by a factor of between four and ten. When the oil crisis really begins to bite, the urban regions using a fraction of fuel of American cities such as Tokyo and Barcelona will undoubtedly be more resilient. On the other hand if U.S., Australian, and Canadian metropolitan regions (the car dependent cities of the world) can improve their resiliency to oil depletion, then the whole world will be more resilient to the problem of peak oil and of course to climate change.[5]

So how do we make car dependent cities more resilient? To understand the approach we are taking, it is necessary to first explain a fundamental theory of how cities work based on the Travel Time Budget.

People in cities on average are willing to travel around half an hour to work and half an hour home again. It has been found to apply in every city in the global sample above and in data on United Kingdom cities for six hundred years. It seems to be related to our need for a space between work and home, but if stretched too far, the time taken for travel begins to undermine our work performance and our ability to contribute to family and community.[6]

Historically this has meant that:

- *Walking Cities* were (and are) dense, mixed-use areas of no more than five kilometers across. These were the major urban form for eight thousand years and in substantial parts of cities like Ho Chi Minh, Mumbai, and Hong Kong, the character of a walking city has been retained. Krakow is mostly a walking city. In wealthy cities like New York, San Francisco, Chicago, London, Vancouver, and Sydney, the central areas are mostly walking cities in character.
- *Transit Cities* from 1850 to 1950 were based on trains and trams, which meant they could spread twenty to thirty kilometers with dense centers and corridors following rail lines and stations. Most European and wealthy Asian cities retain this form, and the old U.S., Australian, and Canadian inner cities also are transit oriented. Many developing cities in Asia, Africa, and Latin America have the dense corridor form of a transit city but don't always have the transit systems to support them; thus they become car-saturated.
- *Automobile Cities* from the early 1950s on; could spread fifty to eighty kilometers in all directions and at low density. U.S., Canadian, Australian, and New Zealand and many new parts of European cities began to develop in this way, but these new areas are reaching the limits of a half hour car commute as they sprawl outward. These are the most vulnerable areas to the oil peak.

In some cities undergoing rapid change like newly developing megacities or rapidly sprawling cities, the travel time budget for an increasing proportion of people can be exceeded. Invariably people will adapt by moving their housing or job or by finding better transportation options. Cities need to adapt to radically reduced car travel, but this will only happen if the travel time budget can be maintained at around an hour a day.

Increasing transit opportunities and accessibility will lead to a rapid decline in car traffic. This can be expected as there is an exponential relationship between increasing transit use and declining car use in the global cities database developed by Jeff Kenworthy. This helps explain why use of cars by inner-city residents in Melbourne is ten times lower than that of fringe residents, though transit use by inner-city residents is only three times greater. The reason is that when people commit to transit, they may sell a car and even move closer to the transit, eventually leading to land use that is considerably less car dependent. In Sydney in 1996, 12 percent of its passenger travel kilometers were on transit. If Sydney invested in doubling its transit patronage it would add another 1,500 pass kms to its system and, using the exponential relationship from Jeff Kenworthy, it would end up reducing car use by over 6,000 pass kms or 61 percent. This would be a dramatic change but is entirely possible in the next 40 years (see resilientcitiesbook.org).

There are many hopeful examples of cities moving in the right direction, and steps that can be taken to reduce our dependency on oil-consuming, greenhouse gas–emitting modes of transportation, while retaining travel-time budgets that are economically and socially realistic. We describe these initiatives below as we map out our vision for more resilient transport.

Seven Elements of a Vision for More Resilient Transport

1. A transit system that is faster than traffic in all major corridors.
2. Viable centers along the corridors that are dense enough to service a good transit system.
3. Walkable areas and cycling facilities that can mean easy access by nonmotorized means, especially in these centers.
4. Services and connectivity that can guarantee access at most times of the day or night without time wasted.

5. Phasing out freeways and phasing in congestion taxes that are directed back into the funding of transit and walk/cycle facilities as well as traffic-calming measures.

6. Continual improvement of vehicle engines to ensure emissions, noise, and fuel consumption are reduced, especially a move to electric vehicles.

7. Regional and local governance that can enable visionary green transport plans and funding schemes to be introduced.

A transit system that is faster than traffic down all major corridors.

Cities need to have a combination of transportation and land-use options that are favorable for green modes and offer a time savings when compared to car travel. This means transit needs to be faster than traffic down each major corridor. Those cities where transit is relatively fast are those with a reasonable level of support for it. The reason is simple—they can save time.

With fast rail systems, the best European and Asian cities with the highest ratio of transit to traffic speeds have achieved a transit option that is faster than the car down the main city corridor. Rail systems are faster in every city in our eighty-four-city sample by ten to twenty kilometers per hour (kph) over bus systems, as buses rarely average over twenty to twenty-five kph. Busways with a designated lane can be quicker than traffic in car-saturated cities (see below), but in lower-density car-dependent cities it is important to use the extra speed of rail to establish an advantage over cars in traffic. This is one of the key reasons why railways are being built in over a hundred U.S. cities.[7]

Rail has a density-inducing effect around stations, which can help to provide the focused centers so critical to overcoming car dependence. Thus transformative change of the kind that is needed to rebuild car-dependent cities comes from new electric rail systems as they provide a faster option than cars and can facilitate the building of transit-oriented centers. If electric rail systems are based on renewable electricity or greenpower, they don't require oil or emit greenhouse gases. Washington, D.C.'s, rail system was built in 1976 as a service for government employees. It has since grown to cover 168 kilometers of track with eighty-six stations and has become a key factor in shaping housing and employment patterns. The Balston corridor has become a global model for transit-oriented development (TOD) planning. In these areas the train is clearly faster than driving. Further expansions to under-served areas such as the auto-only Tyson's Corner, Virginia, are in the planning stage (although the elevated option favored by policymakers for Tyson's Corners will make the creation of TODs challenging).

Paris, like many European cities, has a strong transit system and a walkable central area, but over recent decades it has given over more and more space to the car. Now in a bid to reclaim its public spaces it is implementing a series of policies to reduce the number of cars in the city, but to do so means the alternatives must be quicker and more convenient than cars. They have therefore begun a twenty-year program:

- Creating a neighborhood traffic-calming program (slowing car traffic down) to rival any city in the world
- Building 320 kilometers of dedicated bike lanes
- Developing a new light-rail transit (LRT) system linking a dozen subway and express train lines as it goes around the city, providing cross-city linkages
- Setting aside forty kilometers of dedicated busways (BRT) that enable buses to travel at twice their normal speed and with bus stops that have real time information
- Slowing traffic down on the "red axes," which were once for one-way express traffic but will now be two-way "slow ways" including cycle lanes and narrowed for the provision of more street trees
- Removing every year fifty-five thousand on-street parking spaces
- Working toward a "car free" oasis in the center of Paris that includes all the major iconic buildings and places
- Sinking the Peripherique, the ring road freeway, and covering it with a huge park
- Developing the unique Velib bike share program with twenty thousand "city bikes" in 1450 locations (about every 330 meters across Paris), which can be hired for one Euro per day or by purchasing a weekly, monthly, or annual pass

Eighty percent of Parisians support these innovations.[8]

Bus rapid transit (BRT) is filling a niche in transport between rail and conventional buses. Its main features are enclosed lanes, isolated stops, level boarding, frequent service, large capacity, signal priority, and intelligent control systems. As they can fit onto present road systems they can be cheaper than rail and are considerably cheaper than subways or over-head rail. Ottawa, Curitiba, and Bogotá were the first cities to demonstrate BRTs on a large scale to great acclaim from the transport experts of the world and local citizens. The niche of BRT is that it does not require the infrastructure of rail but has a dedicated thruway; a BRT can carry up to twenty thousand people an hour down its corridors. Buses by themselves in traffic can rarely reach eight thousand people per hour and are very slow. In many third world cities the niche has been filled by thousands of small buses such as mini taxis and these have completely crammed all city streets. BRTs can offer a greener transport option that is faster than traffic or mini taxis.[9]

The limitations to BRT are that bus bunching at the destination points and stations can occur because the time needed to embark and disembark is greater than that needed for trains. Eventually rail capacities of around fifty thousand people per hour (due to size of carriages, speed, and ease of embarkation) are needed in most large cities. This is already happening in Ottawa, Canada, and in Curitiba, Brazil, which are both planning to replace their BRT systems with rail. Unfortunately in Curitiba, which became an icon for demonstrating its BRT in the developing world, the numbers of bus users are declining as the system has reached its limits and people have begun to turn back to their cars. "That competition is very hard," says Paulo Schmidt, the president of URBS, the rapid-bus system. "During peak hours, buses on the main routes are already arriving at almost thirty-second intervals; any more buses, and they would back up." Schmidt has said that a light-rail system is needed to complement it.[10]

Buses can also have emissions and noise problems, which make it more challenging to attract dense development around their stations, though this can be overcome with emissions regulations (especially by favoring CNG) and by noise insulation in buildings.

BRTs are now being developed in Paris, Los Angeles, Pittsburgh, Miami, Boston, Brisbane, Mexico City, Jakarta, Beijing, Kunming, and Chengdu. Many other Chinese cities are now seeing BRT as a much better solution than freeways. As Lee Schipper from EMBARQ and the World Resources Institute says: "If Chinese cities continue the momentum they have gained in the past few years, transport will serve city development, the strangulation by smaller vehicles seen elsewhere will be avoided and Chinese cities will move a large step towards sustainability."[11]

BRTs can also be an excuse for some governments not to fund rail systems. In America many cities are trying to pass ballot measures to raise funds for rail. The usual process of obtaining funds from the U.S. Federal Transit Administration has become almost impossible for rail when there is any chance of BRT since it is significantly cheaper to implement. BRT is often the only option in cities in the developing world. However, for wealthy American cities the situation is different: an alternative to the car must be clearly better. Buses in the past have not provided more efficient solutions for the long term and do not accommodate the development of land around stations. Electric rail systems are likely to be the only solution to provide the kind of resilience needed for the future. Many cities built in the nineteenth century around rail such as European cities and older cities of the United States, Australia, and Latin America still remain in transit city form. However transit systems need to keep pace with their city's growth if they are to respond to peak oil and climate change, thus new rolling stock and new lines into car-dependent suburbs are required to keep the city ahead of the increase in car use.

The biggest challenge in an age of radical resource efficiency requirements will be finding a way to build fast rail systems for the scattered, low-density, car-dependent cities of the world. How can a fast transit service be built into these areas? The solution may well be provided by Perth and Portland, Oregon, which have both built fast rail systems down freeways. To build fast electric rail down the middle of these roads is easier than anywhere else as the right of way is there and engineering in terms of gradients and bridges is compatible. They are not ideal in terms of ability to build TODs but it can still be done using high-rise buildings as sound walls. Linkages from buses, electric bikes, and park and rides are all easily provided so that local travel to the system is short and convenient. In Perth the new Southern Railway has a maximum speed of 130 kph (80 mph) and an average speed of 90 kph (55 mph), which is at least 30 percent faster than traffic. The result is dramatic increases in patronage far beyond the expectations of planners who see such suburbs as too low in density to serve a rail system. There is little else that can compete with this kind of option for creating a future in the car-dependent suburbs of many cities.

While fast electric rail services are not cheap, they cost about the same per mile as most freeways, and we have been able to find massive funding sources for these in the past fifty years. In the transition period it will require some creativity as the systems for funding rail are not as straightforward. In Perth the state government was able to find all the funds from Treasury due to a mining boom. The government was able to pay off the entire rail system, including the new Southern Railway even before it was opened. For most cities it is more difficult (especially in car-dependent U.S. cities) as the funding process has all been about building and maintaining roads. While some progress has been made diverting federal and state funds to transit projects, transportation budgets have been stretched thin as many cities are experiencing an infrastructure crisis and are struggling to maintain and upgrade existing roads and bridges. This was brought into focus by the Minneapolis bridge collapse in 2007.[12]

To solve this funding problem cities have had to find innovative solutions such as financing transit through the use of taxes or direct payments from land development, as in Copenhagen's new rail system, or through a congestion tax as in London (see below).

Funding of transit in congested cities can occur as it has in Hong Kong and Tokyo, where the intensive requirements around stations mean that the transit can be funded almost entirely from land redevelopment. In poorer cities the use of development funds for mass transit can increasingly be justified by the transformation of their urban economy. Peak oil and climate change will become an important part of that rationale.

Viable Centers along Corridors Dense Enough to Service a Good Transit System

In high-density cities such Bangkok, there is no need to think about creating TODs around transit stops, as many of these cities need just to be retrofitted with transit after population and development have exploded. Bangkok has begun to provide a rail rapid transit system that travels through and above its congested streets at over 60 kph while the average traffic speed is 14 kph and the average bus transit speed is just 9 kph.[13]

But in many lower-density urban regions, especially those in the United States, many communities in need of transit do not have the density to make it feasible. Transit needs densities over thirty-five people and jobs per hectare (fourteen per acre) of urban land and for walking/cycling to be dominant requires densities over one hundred people and jobs per hectare (forty per acre). Most new suburbs are rarely more than six or seven people and jobs per acre. Densities in urban areas need to in-

Bangkok's buses, stuck in the traffic. The city could offer a golden opportunity for transit to be faster than car traffic if a guided busway or railway were constructed through its dense corridors. (Credit: Dave Dixon)

crease to support transit and allow more people to live and work where they can have alternative transportation options. Of course it is a chicken and egg situation as often the transit system is needed to get the land-use processes to densify and focus development around stations.[14]

TOD is becoming a guiding philosophy for planners, politicians, and developers as it not only reduces car use by around 50 percent but also saves money on infrastructure and helps create community centers.[15] TODs need to be planned along every transit system so that transit cities are built as an antidote to auto cities. Transit links these centers and provides the regional transport options needed. But within these centers—especially major regional centers—walking and cycling need to be given priority so that it is most efficient to move around for short journeys by these modes. Thus within a TOD is the walking city and it is just as functional in today's economy as in any other period of history. A combination of transit cities and walking cities can be built into an auto city to make it more resilient. Most Australian and Canadian cities are planning this concept as are U.S. cities like Portland and Denver. This idea of walkable, transit-oriented centers is the basis of the New Urbanism, at least in theory.[16]

A study of New Urbanist developments in Perth has revealed some home truths about New Urbanism. Perth has grown rapidly in the past twenty years, and for the past decade many developers have chosen to use a New Urbanist code for development called Livable Neighborhoods and have received key advice from many high-profile New Urbanists such as Peter Calthorpe and Andres Duany. This code ensures that streets are narrower and sidewalks wider, and enables higher-density, mixed-use centers. The study compared eleven New Urbanist developments with forty-six conventional suburbs in the same region of the city. On the positive side, there was a 9 percent switch from cars to walking for local trips in the New Urbanist developments, which came with a reduction in the number of obese people in the New Urbanist suburbs of 7 percent and eight minutes more of physical activity a day on average. This would appear to be related to the straightening out of the road patterns, which makes walking more direct for short trips. However, the New Urbanist developments showed no difference in their regional transport character with identical transport fuel usage per capita as conventional suburbs. The fewer car trips for local travel were washed out by a greater use of cars for longer trips and especially reduced car occupancy. Transit was uniformly very poor for all these suburbs, and when trip times were compared it was found that a transit trip for work would have taken on average over eighty minutes compared to thirty minutes for a car trip. The reality was that none of the New Urbanist suburbs actually produced the density and mix of uses in their centers and hence there just wasn't any better land use or transit service. New Urbanism will be discredited if it cannot actually deliver the kind of land-use and transit options that its rhetoric suggests. New Urbanism must include a strategy of TODs with real transit availability as the way of creating a resilient alternative development mode.[17]

Denver residents took less than 1 percent of their trips by transit in the past twenty years (in spite of having an award-winning bus system), which made it one of the least resilient cities in the world to peak oil. (However, ridership increased 8 percent in the first three months of 2008, in spite of a fare increase. This increase is largely attributed to the cost of fuel.[18]) But this highly car-dependent city is rebuilding itself around six new rail lines. After a twenty-year process of lobbying, the Regional Transportation District's (RTD) Fastracks proposal was put to a referendum in November 2004. The community voted for the proposition to raise $4.7 billion to provide 192 kilometers of new rail track with seventy new stations, thirty kilometers of BRT, and a plan to focus development around the transit system. The transformative plan for Denver is now seen as a national model for dealing with car dependence. One of the keys to its success was the partnership established between political leaders, the RTD, business leaders, NGOs, and neighborhood groups. Most importantly the focus of development now in Denver is around the new rail stations with TODs to supply transit-accessible housing and commerce. The successful delivery of these TODs will determine whether there is an exponential decrease in car use accompanying such transit improvements.[19]

An analysis of how transport fuel use varies across Australian cities has shown three strong relationships with powerful policy implications. First, the closer the development is to the city center the lower the fuel consumption. In fact just knowing how far a development is from the city center can enable one to predict a person's transport fuel or greenhouse gas contribution. This shows how important redevelopment is over fringe development in the post–peak oil city. Second, the higher the density the lower the fuel used. Density could predict fuel use with up to 70 percent certainty in Sydney and again supports the analysis given so far. Third, the quality of the transit service could predict with up to 60 percent certainty how much fuel people were using. Quality transit service was defined as whether an area had a better than fifteen-minute service (with provision on the weekend and evenings). Of course all these physical planning parameters are totally enmeshed in a system of feedback loops, which explains what every ordinary person knows: if you build it they will come; and if you come together then it's easier to build it.[20]

Giving Priority to Pedestrians and Bicyclists in Centers

Nonmotorized transport (NMT)—bikes and walking—need to be given priority over motorized vehicles, especially in dense centers. This can be done by dedicating whole streets to them or by simply making it more equitable for walking and cycling. However, this can only work in dense centers where distances are short enough to walk or cycle.

Whole streets or parts of streets can be set aside for NMT and can be easily justified in terms of the numbers of people assisted in most cities of reasonable density. Some cities are creating a network of green streets where cars and other motor vehicles are banned or significantly constrained. This is the trend now in many European cities, and in part through the work of Danish architect and urban designer Jan Gehl, it has begun to happen in Australian cities and in New York. Gehl has devoted a lifetime of urban design to making Copenhagen a better city through replacing car space with people space and studying how other cities can respond to the same agenda.[21]

In Copenhagen and the Netherlands, where bicycles have continued to be used because the infrastructure was provided for them with cycleways, cities are continuing to expand their systems. In Copenhagen, more than one out of three residents commute by bike, and more than 40 percent commute by bike in Amsterdam. Now whole streets are being set aside for bicycles, and the number of people using bicycles is increasing.[22]

In Vancouver, British Colombia, greener transportation options have shaped the city in significant ways. The population of the city of Vancouver, like many North American downtown areas, began declining in the 1970s and '80s but then began to turn around and has since grown by 135,000 people in the past twenty years. Strong leadership from the city council led this "return to the city" as it established policies to help create quality urban spaces, good cycling and walking facilities, reliable transit (electric rail and electric trolley buses mostly), and most of all high-density residential opportunities with at least 15 percent social housing (public and cooperative housing). This has been so successful that transportation patterns in the city have been transformed. A survey between 1991 and 1994 showed a decline in car trips in the city of Vancouver of 31,000 vehicles per day (from 50 percent to 46 percent of trips), while the amount of cycling and walking went up by a staggering 107,000 trips per day (from 15 percent to 22 percent). In the central area car trips went from 35 percent to 31 percent. The most recent data show that walking and cycling have gone from 15 percent to 30 percent of all trips in a fifteen-year period.

Vancouver has been creating a walking city in its downtown and also in a series of centers along its Sky Train. This policy has been so successful that families are moving back into the city center, so that schools, child care centers, and community centers are crowded, while the number of cars owned in the city has reduced to less than it was in 1999, probably establishing this as a world first, especially in a city undergoing an economic boom. One of the critical policies that has helped make this work is the 5 percent social infrastructure policy whereby the city requires public spaces and social facilities to be provided through each development equal to 5 percent of the cost of the development. Furthermore, the facilities are chosen by the local community, thus overcoming a lot of the "not in my backyard" (NIMBY) reactions from people to higher-den-

In Copenhagen 36 percent of people go to work on a bike compared to just 27 percent by car. (Credit: Timothy Beatley)

sity developments. The walkability of the city or center is the main focus of this investment as people like to have attractive neighborhoods to walk around. These ideas are being incorporated, with significant community input, into a comprehensive eco-density plan for the city of Vancouver. Eco-density is defined as: "an acknowledgement that high quality and strategically located density can make Vancouver more sustainable, livable and affordable."[23]

The priorities in the planning of a city determine its future. A greener urban transport system will be possible if it favors public transport and an NMT system over road building. As the U.S. politicians Paris Glendenning, governor of Maryland, and Christine Todd Whitman, governor of New Jersey (2006) said, "If you design communities for automobiles you get more automobiles. If you design them for people you get walkable, livable communities."

Services and Connectivity That Can Guarantee Frequent Day and Night Access

To enable travel time by alternative transportation modes to be competitive with cars, transit must not only be fast, but service must be efficient

Many new transit-oriented developments have been created around Vancouver's Sky Train. (Credit: iStockphoto.com)

and convenient, and connectivity between various parts of the system must be seamless.[24]

It is possible to replan a city that has inadequate transit so that it is divided into a series of walkable transit cities where local transit services link to faster service down corridors between each walkable transit city. These local transit services can then go across the corridors by linking into stations in a coordinated way from many directions. This is akin to a fractal system. Sydney has restructured its city plan in this way, and this is the basis of Denver's transformative rail project. The centers become the basis of walking and cycling destinations. Thus suburbs that have in the past been disconnected and car dependent can now be integrated into a non–car-based set of sustainable transport options.

These plans are needed to make transit systems work, but in the end the level of service provided will depend on how much the city is willing to spend on its trains and buses. In the next decade as the demand for transit goes up dramatically it will require strong leadership to ensure the sheer quantity of trains and buses is adequate. This will require a reorienting of priorities in transportation funding in all levels of government.

Phasing Out Freeways and Phasing in Congestion Taxes to Fund Sustainable Transport

Freeways are usually proposed to help ease congestion and are considered to save time, fuel, and emissions by avoiding stopping, starting, and idling. Traffic planners use benefit–cost analyses based on these simple ideas to justify the large capital cost of freeways. Will it really save fuel to build freeways? No, the data do not support these contentions. The data show that cities with higher average speeds use more fuel per capita as the faster roads just mean people travel farther and more frequently by car.[25]

Is congestion associated with higher fuel use in cities? No, on the contrary those cities with higher congestion have lower fuel use while cities with the least congestion use the most fuel. Although individual vehicles in less congested cities are moving more efficiently they are being used much more often and for longer distances while greener modes are being used less.[26]

Is removing congestion always a good thing? Not if it is attempted by increasing road capacity; car use will increase to quickly fill the newly available space. The Texas Transportation Institute, in a study of U.S. cities over the past thirty years, found no difference in the levels of congestion between those cities that invested heavily in roads and those that did not. It is possible to make more car dependence and congestion out of a policy designed to improve traffic.[27]

An alternative approach to building freer-flowing traffic systems as a way of saving fuel is to reduce congestion by reducing car use in the city. This was done in Greater London with the bold vision of mayor Ken Livingstone who executed what no one said could be done—a congestion tax. For many years transport economists have recommended that cities tax the use of cars to reduce congestion and pay for the external cost of the motor vehicle. Some smaller attempts have been made in Singapore and Oslo but London was the first major metropolis to attempt a city-wide approach. (New York City has since attempted to implement congestion pricing, which was approved by the city council but not approved by the state legislature.) The London initiative ringed the inner city with sensors that enabled people to pay automatically or to fine those who did not pay when they crossed the cordon into the main part of London. Most importantly the program put the money raised back into better transit. The result was a 15 percent reduction in traffic and much better bus service, both because buses were able to meet their schedules more easily and because there were more of them. The sixty thousand fewer vehicles per day was much preferred by those who chose to continue driving, and 50 to 60 percent of those who stopped driving switched to transit. For the cities of the world, it showed that such intervention can be successful, that you can tax the car to make alternative urban transportation work.[28]

Stockholm found after a six-month trial of the congestion tax that there was a reduction in congestion of 25 percent at the morning rush and 40 percent in the evening; about half the people moved to transit with a 4.5 percent increase in transit patronage (and this from a very high ridership base). A referendum on the issue passed. However, after a conservative government was elected the congestion tax was extended but only if the money earned was ploughed back into new roads. So Stockholm has taken a step backward in the move toward resiliency.[29]

Many western European and Asian cities place an emphasis on creating green transport modes rather than on creating freeways. These cities are among the wealthiest in the world. Latin American and Chinese cities have fifty times less freeways per capita than U.S. cities. When freeways are expressed in terms of meters per dollar of wealth in the city, then sadly the cities that are investing most heavily in freeways relative to their wealth are in Africa and the Middle East. This would indicate a muddled development assistance priority system.[30]

Many cities that have confronted proposed freeways have become global leaders in green transportation—in Europe, Copenhagen and Zurich; in North America, Portland (OR), Milwaukee, Vancouver, and Toronto. These cities were either faced with a new freeway that was ultimately defeated (with the help of Jane Jacobs in Toronto) or tore down an existing freeway that was cutting through the city (Milwaukee) or blocking access to a natural amenity (Portland). The cities opted to provide other greener options such as LRT, green space, cycleways, traffic calming, and associated urban villages, and all have thrived.

The next agenda for cities seriously confronting the oil crisis will be to remove some freeways. In the process of building fast rail down some freeways it is possible to turn the auto-oriented road into a system that is also compatible with biking and walking. This movement is called "Complete Streets." San Francisco decided not to rebuild the elevated Embarcadero Freeway after the Loma Prieta earthquake in 1989. It took three ballots before consensus was reached, but the freeway has been rebuilt as a much more accessible tree-lined boulevard involving light rail and pedestrian and cycle spaces. Traffic calming studies for many years

London's congestion tax has led to 15 percent less traffic with 50 to 60 percent of travelers transferring to transit. (Credit: iStock.com)

have shown that cities adapt and produce less traffic through a range of mechanisms such as changing modes, reducing the numbers of cars that are just cruising (looking for parking or driving for the sake of it), and forcing land use changes that are more compatible with the new traffic capacity. The regeneration of the land uses in the area has followed this change in transportation philosophy.[31]

What these projects have shown is that we should, as David Burwell from the Project for Public Spaces says, "think of transportation as public space."[32] From this perspective, freeways become very unfriendly solutions. However boulevards — with space for cars, cyclists, pedestrians, a busway or LRT, all packaged in good design and with associated land uses that create attractions for everyone — become the gathering spaces that make green cities good cities and that will make them far more resilient in an oil-scarce and climate change–dominated future.

In the United States, the National Complete Streets Coalition is receiving attention for its work to change federal policy to support the creation of streets that "pedestrians, bicyclists, motorists and bus riders of all ages and abilities are able to safely move along and across." In the UK the movement called Naked Streets seeks to reduce the automobile-only orientation of streets, especially by removing all the car-based advertising and traffic signs, meaning that drivers must proceed naked down streets so they slow down. The Demos Institute, a high-profile public policy think tank, has shown how public transport helps create good public spaces, which in turn help define a city. The growing awareness among traffic engineers of this new paradigm for transportation planning is gathering momentum. As Andy Wiley-Schwartz, from Project for Public Spaces, says, "Road engineers are realizing that they are in the community development business and not just in the facilities development business." He calls this the "slow road movement."[33]

Continual Improvement of Vehicle Engines, Especially a Move to Electric Vehicles

For many, particularly those in the United States, the oil issue is only about creating more efficient vehicles. This will not be enough to solve the problem, however. It has not yet diminished vehicle fuel consumption and it is unlikely to do more than make a small contribution in the time required. It will, however, be a necessary part of the solution. It will not of course address issues such as congestion, traffic fatalities, and the mental and social impacts of time lost in single-occupancy vehicles. Increasing vehicle efficiency is only one part of the overall strategy for a more resilient city.

Many commentators look at the theoretical potential of the various transport modes as if they were able to increase their actual passenger loads. Bus loadings, for example, vary enormously though these are not easily improved if a bus route runs through highly dispersed suburbs. The main target is the ridership level in cars—they could carry 4 people instead of the average 1.52—however, this is so universal (it ranges from the lowest occupancy in Geneva and Vienna of 1.2, to the highest in Manila at 2.5) that it would appear to be almost impossible to expect much higher occupancy levels. Indeed, car-pooling has little potential to affect the numbers as it offers a very limited timeframe in the morning and evening commutes. Transit, on the other hand, has a much higher range, from 3.4 in Manila (in their bus jitneys) to 129.3 in Mumbai (per carriage, often with many riders on the roof); so the potential for change in transit occupancy levels appears much more possible; trains can just add more carriages. Record high fuel prices have meant dramatic increases in transit across all cities (10 to 15 percent in many), but not all cities have the extra capacity to expand to the next level of ridership in-

The Complete Streets movement in the United States and the Naked Streets movement in Europe are trying to do the same thing: enable transit users, pedestrians, and cyclists to have just as much right to use a street as a car driver as in this picture of River Street in Santa Cruz, California. (Credit: Glatting Jackson Kercher Anglin, Inc.)

creases, which are expected. No cities seem to be reporting dramatic increases in car pooling.

The other way to improve vehicle fuel efficiency is through improving vehicle technology. However, due to the technological orientation of our age the issue has tended to be shunted off to the engineers to solve. Since the first oil crisis in 1973–74, the solution has been cast as one of creating more technologically efficient cars and trucks. This is still seen by many commentators as the most important response. For example, Jeremy Leggett suggests that U.S. dependence on Middle Eastern oil would be reduced to zero if fuel efficiency were improved in the U.S. vehicle fleet by just 2.7 miles per gallon. This is just 11 percent and yet in 2008 the U.S. was importing 60 percent of its oil, and 21 percent of it came from the Middle East (which must rise as a percentage as other areas are declining). Even if the argument were correct, however, it still assumes people would not drive more if fuel efficiency rose, and, although fuel elasticities are only around 10 to 15 percent, the past few decades have seen people driving more and more in the United States. This is not the fundamental solution to peak oil that we need.[34]

There is no question that vehicle engines have become more efficient in recent decades. For example, in December 2007 President George W. Bush signed into U.S. law the Clean Energy Act of 2007, which requires that automakers increase gas mileage in their vehicles to 35 mpg by 2020. However, increased efficiency has been nullified by the increasing proportion of heavy vehicles and the greater number of vehicles on the road in the United States and Australia. The era of fear has led to the SUV and the Hummer rather than the diminutive fuel-efficient vehicle touted by technological idealists. Thus U.S. vehicle fuel efficiency has reduced from 26.2 mpg in 1987 to 24.4 mpg in 2001, and Australian fleet averages are less than during the 1960s.[35] European and Chinese mileage standards on vehicles are being increased, however, and this is likely to cause ripples throughout the entire vehicle industry.

History will not judge us well that the last decades before peak oil saw *reductions* in fleet fuel efficiency. Huge technological advances exist in vehicle fuel efficiency, they just need to be brought into the mainstream. They alone will never solve the problems of cities, however, all of which require greener transportation solutions.[36]

One of the most pressing reasons for changing fuels and making engines more efficient is the air quality impacts from poor engines. Air quality data from across the world's cities show continuing air quality problems. Vehicle and fuel technology improvements in most developed cities have been successfully able to hold steady or reduce overall ambient air pollution levels despite increases in driving for about twenty years of growth. This is beginning to deteriorate and 121 U.S. cities are now over the air quality standards; this represents 40 percent of the population being exposed to toxic and asthma-causing air.[37]

Regulation is also required at the national and international level to phase out the excessive use of four-wheel drives and other gas guzzlers. But the question should be asked, What is the next best transport technology? The growing consensus seems to be plug-in electric hybrid vehicles (PHEV). PHEVs are now viable alternatives due to the new batteries such as lithium ion, and hybrid engines for extra flexibility. Plug-in electric vehicles must become an important part of a city's electricity grid by enabling renewables to have a storage function. After electric vehicles are recharged at night they can be a part of the peak power provision the next day when they are not being used but are plugged in. Peak power is the expensive part of an electricity system, and suddenly renewables are offering the best and most reliable option. Hence the resilient city is likely to have a significant integration between renewables and electric vehicles through a Smart Grid (as discussed in chapter 4). Electric buses, electric scooters and gophers, and electric cars have an important role in the future resilient city—both in helping to make its buildings renewably powered and in removing the need for oil in transport. Electric rail can also be powered from the sun either through the grid powering the overhead wires or in the form of new light rail (with these new Li-ion batteries), which could be built down highways into new suburbs without requiring overhead wires. Signs that this transition to electric transport is underway are appearing in demonstration projects such as Google's 1.6 MW solar campus in California (with 100 PHEVs) and by the fact that oil companies are acquiring electric utilities.[38]

What sort of impact could there be? According to one study the integration of hybrid cars with the electric power grid could reduce gasoline consumption by 85 billion gallons per year. That is equal to

27 percent reduction in total U.S. greenhouse gases
52 percent reduction in oil imports
$270 billion not spent on gasoline[39]

The real test of a resilient city will be how it integrates these electric vehicles and electric transit.

Strong Regional and Local Governance and Strong Citizen Support to Enable Visionary Green Transport

Cities are organisms that work as a whole regional system and as a series of local parts. They need viable governance systems at both the regional and the local level to create green transportation options for more resilient cities.

Visionary master plans and regional governance structures enabled governments to build the urban freeways of the auto city. Today, cities need new visionary plans to generate the political momentum and find the funds for oil-proofing their cities, as well as the governance structures that can carry out the plans. Regional governance structures for transportation exist in most cities in Canada and Australia and to a lesser extent in the United States.[40]

Bogotá and Curitiba relied on regional governance systems, city money, and World Bank support to build their transformative transit systems. Mumbai and Kolkata also have a regional governance system that manages their massive transit systems. Megacities without such a system will find regional transit difficult, and U.S. cities will have to overcome their multitudes of local government in each city-region to create coherent regional plans. Regional planning has become very successful in Portland through a statutory process established by the State of Oregon. Similar processes could happen to bring the voluntary networks of local governments and the nascent metropolitan planning organizations into a more coherent future.[41]

Regional transit systems cannot work unless local systems feed into them. Local governments, citizens, and businesses need to come up with their own peak oil and climate change plans, since each part of a city has different economic functions. The cities that have done best at building regional transit systems—Zurich, Munich, Hong Kong, Singapore, and Tokyo—also have active local transport planning processes. Zurich allows each canton to choose the timetable they require for their transit.

Surveys constantly show that people want to see greener transportation options given higher priority in their cities. In Perth, people were asked if they saw a need for more transit, walking, and biking over cars, and 78 percent agreed they did; then they were asked if they would transfer road funding to pay for these greener modes, and 87 percent agreed with that idea. Such views emboldened the government to transfer priorities; they switched from a 1:5 ratio of transit spending to roads spending to a 5:1 ratio, and the resulting rail system has increased patronage from 7 to 50 million passengers in fifteen years. This platform has been used to win four state elections. In 2007 the Southern Rail was opened with 90 percent support rates and was so popular the government was able to pay off its debt before the rail system even opened. In Porto Alegre, Brazil, a people's budget approach asked citizens to assign priorities for expenditures; the vast majority of neighborhoods put greener modes of transportation above the need for more roads. In Milwaukee, Wisconsin, a survey showed that bus and rail projects were favored by 70 to 85 percent of those surveyed, whereas "more highway capacity" came in last, with 59 percent support. A gasoline tax was the preferred way to pay for such improvements. And in Oregon, the Transportation Priorities Project showed similar sentiments about transit over freeway options.[42]

In the past, transportation priorities have generally been set by policymakers and engineers, not the public. But in the United States and elsewhere voters are starting to send the clear message that they want better options and are willing to pay for them. Between 2000 and 2006, voters in thirty-three states approved over 70 percent of transport ballot measures, generating more than $110 billion in investments—much of it for public transportation.

The U.S. system for funding transportation requires that metropolitan regions develop a set of priorities through a Metropolitan Planning Organization (MPO) that can then apply through the state for federal funds. This model could be extended to all aspects of the resilient cities agenda to provide the core governance for funding the transition to less

Perth opens its Southern Rail with 90 percent approval ratings and 50,000 boardings a day; the State Government was able to pay off the debt on the railway before it was even open; new TODs like the one on the Perth foreshore replacing a freeway are now feasible and attractive to the public.

petroleum-dependent cities. This idea is explored in the final chapter as a key way to bring about integrated solutions.

Will These Changes Bring Exponential Decline in Fuel Use?

What then can we expect if we introduce vehicle and fuel changes as suggested and also build good transit systems? Will these kinds of technological changes and land use changes help bring about the resilient cities we need? Will they start the exponential decline in fuel use that we require? We believe that support for the types of policies referenced above can begin to reverse decades of car-oriented planning.

Conclusions

Cities need visions about how they can be transformed to confront peak oil and climate change by overcoming car dependence and switching to renewable fuels. And they need strong, forward-thinking political leaders who can overcome the various barriers that prevent these visions from coming true. This chapter will conclude by making some comments about Perth and Portland—two very car dependent cities that have begun the transition back to resilience. They are remarkably similar stories that offer some hope that car-based cities can come back from the brink.

Portland and Perth are West Coast cities based around resource extraction with "Wild West" pasts. During the postwar period they both went the way of most cities—to become shaped by the car. Both cities had painful political confrontations in the 1970s involving freeways that would have been highly destructive. Both chose instead, after successful citizen-led campaigns, to build a rail system to see if that could provide some options for their future. In the past twenty years the rail system of Portland has been extended some 44 miles with 64 stations and has gone to 34 million passengers a year. In Perth, the rail system has extended 108 miles with thirty-two stations and now carries around 50 million passengers a year. Moreover, the number of commuters using transit has risen from 5 percent to 10 percent in the ten years from 1996. These are both transit success stories in cities that were not really dense enough at the time for most transport planners to consider rail viable.

The land use patterns in Portland and Perth were changed by these decisions. Both cities have around twenty active TODs being built with considerable interest from developers as the market for walkable, dense, mixed-use developments has skyrocketed. Both cities have strong regional governance that can facilitate this more resilient urban form. But the driving force behind both cities has been a highly aware and politically active citizenry that has demanded options in light of peak oil and climate change.

In Perth the importance of the TravelSmart program in helping to bring about this cultural transition should not be underestimated. More than a third of the population of Perth has been visited by a TravelSmart officer and provided with personalized advice about how to use their cars less and be more oriented to transit, biking, and walking. The results show that over 15 percent have become less car dependent. The political impetus that is generated is what drives results such as the extraordinary turnaround in funding and the 90 percent support for the new Southern Railway. Portland has also used TravelSmart and a range of other community engagements over the years that have helped sway the public to vote for a more resilient city.

Thus we turn to the final chapter with a sense that if two highly car dependent cities can move toward greater resilience, then perhaps any city can.

6

Conclusion: Ten Strategic Steps toward a Resilient City

Resilient cities can be created out of the challenge of peak oil and climate change. We have provided models from some cities striving to achieve exponential decline in car use and develop new renewably based energy to power buildings and transport. This chapter seeks to draw together the visions of hope with some practical strategies for moving cities toward greater resiliency. These strategies need to involve all parts of the community—government, business, professional practitioners, community groups, and individual households.

Ten strategies are suggested:

Set the vision, prepare an implementation strategy.
Learn on the job.
Target public buildings, parking, and road structures as green icons.
Build TOD, POD, and GOD together.
Transition to resilient infrastructure step by step.
Use prices to drive change where possible.
Rethink rural regions with reduced oil dependence.
Regenerate households and neighborhoods.
Facilitate localism.
Use approvals to regulate for the post-oil transition.

Set the Vision, Prepare an Implementation Strategy

Cities need peak oil and climate change resilience strategies to guide them through the necessary changes, including infrastructure spending, especially on transit for the outer suburbs, new planning systems for how to restructure the city to reduce vehicle miles traveled (VMT) and overall energy consumption (such as Smart Grids), new regulations for energy-efficient buildings and vehicles, and household-based awareness campaigns.

Awareness of climate change is high, while general acceptance of peak oil is low as it is easier to blame oil companies, speculators, banks, and OPEC rather than take the unpopular political stand that we need to consume less and find alternatives to oil. The response to peak oil and climate change must be addressed simultaneously as the demand and supply issues begin to cross over. Global conferences of nations need to be established through the UN and other regional groupings like APEC (the Asia Pacific Economic Cooperation) in order to set goals and begin sharing information on how the world economy can be weaned off oil. Every level of government needs to become involved in these strategies, especially the level of government closest to cities. States, regions, and cities need to create a vision of how they will lessen their dependence on oil and lower carbon emissions..

The city of Brisbane in Queensland has developed a peak oil and climate change strategy that could become a model for any city. The city covers a large part of the Brisbane region but not all, so it still needs the rest of the SE Queensland Region (SEQ) to join its strategy. The strategy development taskforce, which consisted of university, business, and NGO leaders, conducted a series of community engagements before presenting its report in March 2007. The report shows how important action is to prepare the city but also sees it as a significant opportunity for new jobs related to this response. The report includes thirty-one recommendations across eight strategy areas including leadership and partnering, decision making, communication, planning, sustainable transport, preparedness for change, diversification of natural resources, and research. It sets a goal of zero net greenhouse gas emissions by 2050 (with households being carbon neutral by 2020). Steps have been taken to achieve this goal, such as the implementation of strong regulations on energy efficiency, increased investment in renewables, commitment to a regional carbon sink, and emphasis on TOD (transit-oriented development) and TDM (travel demand management) to ensure transport is a priority. The taskforce also presented a package of "20 by 2020" goals that are intended to serve as a guide (and were not formally adopted):

20 percent of transport fuels from non-petroleum sources (n.b., the taskforce ultimately recommended a more stringent target than this)

20 percent of electricity from renewable sources
Additional 20 percent vegetation cover for the region
20 percent of domestic water from rain or "gray water"
20 percent absolute reduction in water consumption
20 percent increase in residential density across the region
Additional 20 percent of houses using solar or gas hot water
20 percent of urban travel on public transport
20 percent of urban trips on bicycle or foot
20 percent of central business district road space pedestrianized.[1]

Strategies for the transition away from oil dependency must be based on partnerships between government, business, and civil society. This partnership approach was demonstrated in Canada by the City of Hamilton's energy strategy, which resulted in the Partners for Climate Protection (PCP).[2]

Passing a resolution acknowledging peak oil and climate change is a critical first step in moving toward resiliency, but the resolutions need to be followed by a plan for implementing change. This has been the criticism of cities signing onto the Mayor's Climate Change Initiative and nations that have signed onto Kyoto. This will eventually become a major political problem as oil and natural gas prices continue to rise and few options for change are apparent.

Some policymakers are beginning to take serious steps toward implementing carbon-cutting measures. In 2008 London mayor Ken Livingstone committed to cutting carbon emissions in London's public buildings by 25 percent by bringing in energy companies to assure these energy savings. When announcing the program Mayor Livingstone said, "Today marks the start of the transformation of London's buildings from the major source of carbon emissions in the city, to a beacon of modern, low-carbon efficiency."[3]

Before an effective implementation plan can be created, an analysis must be done of what it will take to change how we build and where and how people move around city regions. While this is no small task, existing initiatives provide some insight, and there is a growing number of tools available to local governments for creating and implementing a strategic plan ,including a new guidebook created by the group Post Carbon Cities[4] and resources offered by initiatives such as the Clinton Climate Leadership Group (www.c40cities.org, working with Mayor Livingstone, Mayor Bloomberg, and others), and ICLEI (www.iclei.org, which partnered with

Hamilton, Ontario, Canada, and numerous other groups worldwide). The Congress for the New Urbanism, an urban design group that has long advocated for walkable, mixed-use communities, offers a ten-step strategy for reducing our automobile dependency (see cnu.org). The Brookings Institution, a nonprofit public policy organization, offers a policy agenda for reducing carbon emissions in metropolitan areas (www.brookings.edu).[5] There are also local initiatives of national groups such as the Sierra Club New York's "Beyond Oil," which seeks to help New York prepare for high fuel prices and adapt to climate change (beyondoilnyc.org).

A peak oil and climate change resilience strategy cannot be achieved without full public participation. Participatory processes have been well documented and demonstrated across the globe. The processes used to engage the public in the development of the strategic plan for Perth, the State Sustainability Strategy, and the Dialogue for the City were based on the America Speaks model, which was used in the 9/11 consultations and in other U.S. cities since (see www.Americaspeaks.org). The value of these engagement processes cannot be underestimated as the community in the end has to support the long-term vision or it is meaningless.[6]

Embracing a resilient city agenda in response to peak oil requires elected officials to think outside the box and to be motivated by a genuine concern about impacts and future outcomes that will likely extend beyond the typical two-, four-, or six-year electoral cycle. Political courage, strong leadership, and knowledgeable officials are all required, though they are perhaps in short supply. What is needed is a new politics that values the future; understands the importance of stimulating, underwriting, and nurturing new transit systems and renewable energy technologies and markets; and views forging a new energy path as a legitimate function for all levels of government (especially the local level).

These visions can be integrated and work well together, enabling synergies and partnerships to be generated. This forms the basis of hope.

Learn on the Job

The processes of working out how to make a more resilient, sustainable solar city will require learning on the job. The city of Freiburg calls it "Learning by Planning," and they must have learned a lot in the development of Vauban where they created a whole new approach to sustainable urban development by setting strong goals and then asking an

NGO (Forum Vauban) to do the implementation. Frieburg knew there was no model for how to make a car-free carbon neutral city; they had to invent it. In academic circles this approach to new ways of governing is called policy learning. It is not new to say that integrated, interdisciplinary solutions are the best way to tackle difficult and complex problems. It is new, however, to create processes that allow space in the decision-making process for this to occur. The space in the system is critical as professionals need to be able to go beyond their specializations to consider deeper issues where nobody tends to go. In any project this means you need time to understand any policy learning that is thrown up by the process.

The genius of the Frieburg process was that they understood the value of involving the community, and this gave those involved a chance to reflect on the value of the framework they were using to solve the problem. Real innovation then had a chance to emerge, and professionals were able to provide advice as they learned on the job.[7]

This is particularly important when there are deeper social issues underlying projects such as the conflict between the "descriptive" sciences and engineering, which collect data on issues, and the "interpretive" arts, which involve worldviews and values. The clashes between engineers and planners are legendary and have the potential to increase as we deal with the uncharted territory of the resilient city. As Bradbury and Raynor say, we need to "reconcile the irreconcilable." When space is created for technical experts to interact with the community and experts in other fields, the new perspectives often lead to new solutions.[8]

The professional practices of engineering, town planning, and environmental conservation all began with a strong ethical direction as the problems of cities demanded solutions in the nineteenth century. This ethical dimension has had to be played down as professionals developed status and credibility in boardrooms and government committees. The use of manuals and standards, accreditation, and much talk about "best practices" are often all that is allowed. Such a process will inevitably continue as the dominant paradigm of professionalism. But the complexity of sustainability and resilience at this stage in our history demands more. If we are to rely on the manuals and standards of the past then we will not solve the big issues we face. Peak oil and decarbonizing the economy will roll over our cities and we will not be ready or able to respond at the professional level. Younger professionals are increasingly breaking these molds, and whole new approaches are now being taken by consulting firms such as Parsons Brinckerhoff, Arup, GHD, and Maunsells as they see the requirements of the sustainability transition. The new cutting edge in sustainability is coming from these firms as they learn on the job.[9]

Target Public Buildings, Parking, and Road Structures as Green Icons

Municipal and state authorities can respond to the need for more sustainable transport and solar building by first examining the land and buildings that they have control over. In chapter 4, we saw an iconic and innovative government approach to energy-efficient building in Melbourne's CH2 building, which exports solar energy and mines the sewer for water. In the same way, policymakers can demonstrate leadership in renewably powered transport vehicles such as Stockholm's biogas trucks and cars powered from sewage or Calgary's wind-powered light rail.

The most dramatic way a city can demonstrate a commitment to reducing car dependence is by taking a strategic approach to key areas of public space that have been given over to the automobile, namely parking and road space. In any city about one third of its space is tarmac for the automobile. All this space dedicated to parking costs money and is simply unproductive land, but very few cities have sought to demonstrate how it can be better used in a de-carbonizing, post–peak oil world.

Every year for the last thirty years the city of Copenhagen has removed 2 percent of its parking space from streets and squares and created pedestrian areas. Each year the city has grown in its cycling and walking (now 36 percent of the modal split), and car use has declined (now 27 percent). Yet the city has become more popular as a place to live and work and has grown in its ability to create wealth through services. The number of people sitting in the squares and pedestrian areas has grown consistently as the car parking spaces have been removed.[10]

Seoul, Korea, removed a large freeway from its city center that had been built over a major river. The freeway became controversial because of the blighting impacts on the built environment and the destruction of the river. Now the city delights in a six km long urban park along a restored river, and the traffic has virtually disappeared as mass transit and traffic calming have reduced it. Other car-saturated Asian cities are planning to replace their central city freeways, and in Aarhus, Denmark, the city dug up a major arterial to reveal the Aarhus River and created a won-

Copenhagen—arguably the most walkable and cycling-friendly city in the world reached this status by step-by-step reductions in parking, slowly reclaiming roads for public spaces. (Credit: Timothy Beatley)

derful public space along its banks. Perhaps an indicator of a city's resilience potential will be the number of kilometers of pedestrian spaces and green spaces replacing urban roads.

Similar projects are underway in the United States (with the Complete Streets movement, for example), and in New York City, which is creating new public spaces in every community, as well as the many projects documented by the Project for Public Spaces (see pps.org).

The symbolic and economically practical advantages of removing auto-only infrastructure and building transit capacity and walkability have now been established in quite a few cities, but the largely scattered outer suburbs built around the car still depend heavily on freeways. This can change. The provision of a fast rail service down freeways to struggling outer suburbs may become a vital priority for their economic survival in an age of peak oil and climate change pressure on fuel use.

Build TOD, POD, and GOD Together

Transit-oriented development (TOD) has become an important technique for reducing automobile dependence. A 2008 study by the Center

Aarhus River is revealed as part of a new city public space project replacing an arterial road. (Credit: Jan Gehl)

for Transit Oriented Development shows that people in TODs drive 50 percent less than those in conventional suburbs. In both Australia and the U.S., homes that are located in TODs are holding their value the best or have appreciated the fastest under the pressure of rising fuel prices. The Urban Land Institute 2008 report, "Emerging Trends in Real Estate," also suggests that TODs appreciate fastest in up markets and hold value better in down markets.[11] For the full agenda of sustainability to be addressed TODs need to also be pedestrian-oriented developments (PODs) and green-oriented developments (GODs).

The facilitation of TODs has been recognized by all Australian cities and many American cities in their metropolitan strategies, which have developed policies to reduce car dependence through centers along corridors of quality transit. The major need for TODs is not in the inner areas, where services and housing are likely to already surround transit stops. However, in the newer outlying suburbs, built in the past four or five decades, TODs may not exist or transit may just be in the planning phase. This raises many equity issues as the poor increasingly are trapped on the fringe with high expenditures on transport. Affordable housing is an important consideration for inclusion in TODs.

There is significant pent-up demand for TODs in the U.S. as shown in a study done by the Center for Transit Oriented Development. In a detailed survey across several states, the Center assessed that the market for people wanting to live within half a mile of a TOD was 14.6 million households. This is more than double the number who currently live in TODs. The market is based on the fact that those living in TODs now (who were found to be smaller households, the same age, and the same income on average as those not in a TOD) save some 20 percent of their household income by not having to own so many cars—those in TODs owned 0.9 cars per household compared to 1.6 for households not in TODs. This saves on average $4,000 to $5,000 per year per household.[12] In Australia a similar calculation showed this would save some $750,000 in superannuation over a lifetime. Most importantly, this extra income is likely to be spent locally on urban services, which means the TOD approach is a local economic development mechanism.

TODs must also be PODs, that is, pedestrian-oriented developments, or they lose their key quality as a car-free environment where businesses and households are attracted. This will not happen automatically and requires the close attention of urban designers. Jan Gehl's transformations of central areas such as Copenhagen and Melbourne are showing the principles of how to improve TOD spaces so they are more walkable, economically viable, socially attractive, and environmentally significant.[13] It will be important for those green developers wanting to claim credibility that scattered urban developments no matter how green in their buildings and renewable infrastructure, will be seen as failures in a post–peak oil world unless they are building pedestrian-friendly TODs.

At the same time, TODs that have been well designed as PODs will also need to be GODs—green-oriented developments. TODs will need to ensure that they have full solar orientation, are renewably powered, have water-sensitive design, use recycled and low-impact materials, and include innovations such as green roofs.

Perhaps the best example of a TOD-POD-GOD is the redevelopment of Kogarah Town Square in Sydney. This inner city development is built upon a large city council car park adjacent to the main train station, which had a collection of poorly performing businesses nearby. The site is now a thriving mixed-use development consisting of 194 residences, fifty thousand square feet of office and retail space, and thirty-five thousand square feet of community space including a public library and town square. The buildings are oriented for maximum use of the sun with solar shelves on each window (enabling shade in summer and deeper penetration of light into each room), photovoltaic (PV) collectors were installed on the roofs, all rain water is collected in an underground tank to be reused in toilet flushing and irrigation of the gardens, recycled and low impact materials were used in construction, and all residents, workers, and visitors to the site have a short walk to the train station (which allowed for a reduction in parking requirements). Compared to a conventional development, Kogarah Town Square saves 42 percent of the water and 385 tons of greenhouse gas—this does not include transport oil savings, which are hard to estimate but are likely to be even more substantial.[14]

While the demand for TODs is growing, creating TODs can still present significant challenges given the complexity of financing them and the number of private and public actors involved. It has been suggested in Perth that the twenty or so TODs in the planning stages should adhere to a new TOD zoning requirement that mandates minimal amounts of parking, maximum density and mix, the inclusion of green innovations, and a minimum of 15 percent affordable housing.

Ellen Greenberg, director of policy and research for CNU, suggests a six-step planning and policy approach to implementing TODs: create customized zoning for projects integrating transit facilities, minimize customized planning and discretionary review for standardized projects, provide an explicit foundation in policy and politics, engage transit organization policy leadership, meet multiple objectives (e.g., affordable housing, commuter parking, transit transfer station, meeting carbon reduction goals), and anticipate a lengthy timeline for customized projects.[15]

TODs can be built as public–private partnerships (PPPs) because there is a shared value to the agency running the transit as well as the extra real estate value to the developer of land around a station. In Chatswood, Sydney, the first "value transfer PPP" has been successfully completed. The air rights to the station were granted to a developer of a new retail and residential complex on the site, who in exchange was required to build a new station precinct. By stringing together a series of potential TODs it is also possible to find most of the money to support a new rail system that is needed to make the TODs work. Portland's new street car line was built this way. TOD entrepreneurship will be an important part of creating a resilient city.[16]

Kogarah Square in Sydney, one of the few TODs that is also a POD and a GOD. (Credit: City of Kogarah)

Transition to Resilient Infrastructure Step by Step

Resilience requires that infrastructure (road, sewer, water, buildings, transit) in cities is repaired, improved, and expanded. The real challenge is to do this in ways that are "transformative" not just "incremental" otherwise the task just gets bigger and bigger. We need transformative resilient infrastructure for transport and for buildings as integrated packages. Can they be done together?

Two new projects in the United States show that the development community is ready to try innovative and transformative projects. These are the redevelopment of the Austin Mueller Airport (see Web site resilientcities.org) and the redevelopment of Treasure Island in San Francisco. Treasure Island is a human-made island created in the 1930s for the Golden Gate International Exposition and later used as a naval base. It is in the middle of the San Francisco Bay and has very limited road accessibility since its main egress is from the Bay Bridge. The redevelopment plan for the island includes housing for ten thousand people. The community will be linked to the city by a ferry; local buses, electric gophers, and shared electric cars will provide easy access around the island;

and there will be limited parking available in structures located away from the residential area (as in Vauban). An educational program will help to ensure that residents are culturally attuned to the new style of urban living without heavy reliance on the automobile. This is an opportunity to create a much more self-sufficient community with the density and mix of uses where most services can be provided locally. The project will also have the highest-level green buildings and will be committed to renewable energy and carbon neutral power and heating/cooling provision with a Smart Grid. The electric car sharing vehicles and local electric gophers will be fed off the renewable power. Thirty percent of the housing will be affordable. Treasure Island is linked to the small Yerba Buena Island, and plans are in place to restore the heritage and habitat there.

The substantial infrastructure funding required for the transition to a more resilient city is often achieved through a partnership between different levels of government and the private sector. Such a public–private partnership process was developed in the United States for transport, but it does not generally address all the dimensions of resilience required. Instead of just approving funds for transit systems, for example, it may be better to generate resilient city funds that link transit with TOD-POD-GOD type developments. Thus, instead of cities like Denver receiving funds only to build their $5 billion new rail system, which with its six new lines promises to be quite transformative, it would be possible to fund a series of demonstration TOD-POD-GODs along the rail system, giving clear direction as to how the resilient city is being rebuilt with green buildings, renewable energy resources, and reduced car dependence.

Perth's new rail system, which has been built with substantial political input over the past fifteen years, is also quite transformative in terms of transport but not yet in the TOD-POD-GOD agenda. It has cost $2 billion and has given the city a 180-kilometer modern electric rail system with seventy-two stations; it was built with no federal funds, though the freeway it uses as right of way was funded almost entirely from federal sources. This railway has been justified over many elections as a way of oil-proofing the city. As mentioned earlier, the southern rail line was opened in December 2007 with 90 percent support ratings and was fully paid off before it even ran. It became a powerful symbol of hope for Perth in an oil-sensitive future. There are many new developments planned around its stations to take advantage of this opportunity and its obvious

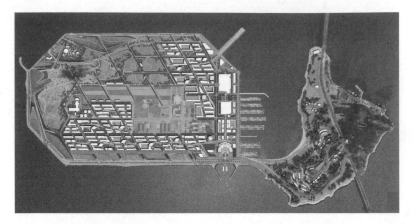

Treasure Island—artist's drawing of the new green city. (Credit: Arup, San Francisco)

amenity now, but there is still much of Perth (like most cities built in the era of car dependence) that remains highly vulnerable to peak oil. A sustainable cities fund that could help build transformative green urbanism around the new stations would be the really important next sign of hope.

Some potential for this kind of change in Australia has come in the House of Representatives Report on Sustainable Cities, which came out in 2005 and recommends that infrastructure funds (especially for rail) be provided for cities, especially in the middle and outer suburbs. In 2008 federal funding programs through Infrastructure Australia are being developed after years of neglecting the cities, and attempts to direct this into achieving climate change and peak oil innovations have been flagged.

What is needed most is for transport infrastructure and power infrastructure funding to be linked into a resilient cities infrastructure program that requires green buildings and green power systems that are fully integrated into innovative electric transit systems and electric vehicles through Smart Grids. This would build on the TOD, POD, and GOD ideas outlined above and would lead to the transformative changes in energy as well as transport. They would need to demonstrate large-scale savings in oil and greenhouse gases before being funded.

Bill Lucy and David Phillips from the University of Virginia have proposed a similar Sustainable Regional Incentive Fund in the United States to work as a way of bringing cities and counties together in confronting their long-term prospects, such as dealing with peak oil and climate change. The Regional Plan Association of New York–New Jersey–

Connecticut has suggested a regional fund to support regional planning, especially around transit. Such funds can reward those cities and regions achieving more sustainable outcomes and thus act as an incentive for cities to work toward an oil-free future.[17]

In Australia the House of Representatives Environment Committee has recommended a similar model. They suggest that the necessary infrastructure for water, power, and transport for the transition to sustainability should occur through the creation of a set of federal sustainability outcomes that states need to achieve. These outcomes would be set by a National Sustainability Commission based on an agreed upon Sustainability Charter. If states met their agreed outcomes in reduced water, power, and oil, then they would be rewarded with more funds and if they do not then they would be fined. This model has worked for policy related to utilities through a National Competition Commission. It can be translated into a powerful mechanism that generates real transformative momentum for change at local, regional, and state levels. The projects of the resilient cities infrastructure program would be all strong symbols of hope as cities began to face the challenges of resilience in a carbon-constrained future.

Use Prices to Drive Change Where Possible

One of the main characteristics of our modern society is that so many of the direct and indirect consequences of our consumption and other personal (and collective) decisions are hidden from us. We tend to judge our investments in renewable energy in terms of artificially truncated, incomplete pricing systems that fail to adequately account for the full and true costs of our overuse of fossil fuels.

Buying a house in auto-dependent suburbs, far away from work and commerce, does not include the full costs of commuting—economic costs or cost to the environment and human health. Numerous studies show the hidden costs of such sprawling development to governments and to individuals. One study that compares the costs of alternative development patterns found that smart growth could provide savings of anywhere from five to seventy-five thousand dollars annually per unit for public infrastructure costs and five hundred to ten thousand dollars annually per unit for incremental operations, maintenance, and service costs.[18]

Another calculation based on Australian cities shows that for every 1,000 dwellings built in TODs rather than as fringe development, $86

million would be saved in up-front infrastructure costs (to government utilities) and $250 million would be saved in transport costs to the individuals
living in the TODs annualized over 50 years. This would be associated
with reductions of 4,500 tons of greenhouse emissions per year for the
1,000 dwellings and health savings of approximately $2.3 million per year
due to better physical health and fewer incidences of depression associated with excessive car use.[19] Most of the energy we use does not include
the costs of pollution, the costs of greenhouse-induced climate change, or
the cost of oil vulnerability and subsequent foreign policy responses. The
price of petroleum and driving is a very good example. Most people consider driving to be cheaper than transit. However, data suggest that direct
costs are more when they are totaled (though these are rarely tallied as
gasoline alone is seen as the cost) and when external costs (such as building and maintaining road infrastructure and the cost to the individual of
purchasing and maintaining an automobile) are added, driving is much
more expensive. The costs of car travel have been estimated to be about
three times the cost of transit, though it is perceived by motorists to be less
expensive.[20] This would suggest that creating a more resilient city with 25
to 50 percent less car use derived from a combination of new transit and
TODs would in fact create a more economically resilient city. Evidence to
support this is now becoming clear. Transit-based cities spend around 5 to
8 percent of their city wealth on transportation but in heavily car-based
cities this ranges from 12 to 15 percent (even 19 percent for Phoenix).[21]

If enhancing human health, reducing oil dependency, and lessening
greenhouse gas emissions are not reason enough to consider changing or
adapting our infrastructure to be more resilient, policymakers need to
assess the long-term financial savings of transit and compact TODs.

The economic benefits of greening urban transportation are beginning to be seen by some parts of the normally car-oriented conservative
side of politics. According to the Washington lobby group The Free Congress Foundation: "Conservatives tend to assume that transit does not
serve any important conservative goals. But it does. One of the most important conservative goals is economic growth. In city after city, new rail
transit lines have brought higher property values, more customers for
local businesses and new development."[22]

Pricing is a useful public policy wherever it can be done to achieve
positive economic outcomes. Also, pricing will inevitably help expose
the unsustainable subsidies to cars and fossil fuels. The opportunities like
the congestion tax in London are rare as taxing driving is politically very

unpopular. However, these opportunities must be grasped whenever possible in cities with heavy regional congestion. As pricing schemes such as this one are successful in more cities, it will be easier politically to implement them elsewhere. Such cities will grow in their ability to respond to the resilience agenda.

While renewable energy technology is becoming ever more cost effective, it often still appears to be uncompetitive with power from coal. However, the new Smart Grid with renewables and battery storage in electric vehicles means that renewable power should not be compared to base load coal power but to the much more expensive top up power sources like gas and even distillates, which are used for peak power. Renewables like wind and solar power can feed into the grid at times of peak use. The economics of this are very favorable.[23]

Renewable energy needs financial incentives to induce or encourage its use. There are many solar incentives that have been applied: buy-downs for rooftop PV systems; feed-in tariffs that mean the PV or wind owner can receive more for the renewable power that they push back into the system than it costs to receive from the grid; production credits (e.g., for wind power), tax credits for hybrid cars; solar and energy efficient mortgages, among many others. And of course raising the relative price of fossil fuels is an equally important signal through the removal of fossil fuel subsidies. Carbon taxes and generally higher energy taxes in European countries (and cities) represent perhaps the best and most productive example of this.

Renewable energy in almost any form — in both rural and urban contexts — suffers from what might be called a "payback ethic," holding essentially that any significant financial investment must demonstrate a clear and certain, and ideally short, time before savings or benefits will cover the investment. While such economic reasoning prevails in many policy and planning spheres, it appears particularly prevalent when applied to transit systems, PVs, biomass, wind energy, and other renewable energy technologies. Yet, had similar narrow, short-term thinking been universally applied, very few investments in, indeed very few qualities of, most cities would exist today. Long-term investments in public transit, public art and public spaces, education, music and culture, parks and environmental quality, to name a few, are the result of a public ethic or ethos that recognizes the need to make expenditures for the long-term good of society; the decisions were not, and should not be, based on a short-term economic calculation.

Rethink Rural Regions with Reduced Oil Dependence

Rural regions have become more productive in the age of cheap oil, though mostly with reduced populations. Can peak oil and climate change offer opportunities to create a better future for these regions? Can city-regional strategies begin to provide hope for rural regions?

Cities cannot exist without their bioregions that they depend on for food, fiber, recreational, and ecological services.[24] Each city and its rural region needs to examine their contribution to climate change and what it will mean for them if less oil is available. As few cities have peak oil and climate change strategies it is probably no surprise to find that even fewer rural regions around cities have such strategies.

One exception is found in Western Australia where the first Regional Sustainability Strategy has been completed in the remote Pilbara region.[25] The Pilbara region produces nearly 20 percent of the world's iron ore and also exports liquefied natural gas (LNG) from its large reserves. The strategy suggests among other things that the Pilbara should become a demonstration region for how to become diesel free. The Pilbara is well set up for this as it is in a period of growth, which is bringing considerable investment to the area. And it has substantial resources of natural gas, which seems to be the best short-term transition fuel to replace oil. Yet all the big trucks, mining equipment, and rail systems are powered by diesel and even the power stations are mostly fueled by diesel—largely imported from the Middle East. Technology exists for all of these systems to be transferred to run on local gas, especially through CNG (compressed natural gas). Indeed the use of natural gas is an obvious replacement for all freight vehicles in areas where gas supplies are adequate. Paybacks for these investments of around two to three years are being found with current fuel prices. A major partnership program should create a large experiment to demonstrate how to convert one of the world's highest solar insolation rates into electricity to electrolyze water into hydrogen, eventually feeding this into the pipelines and liquefaction plants that are there. Then eventually Perth and the whole region could be fed with a hydrogen source provided from solar energy in its northern region rather than natural gas.

A number of mining companies in the Pilbara are now looking at how they can move to being "carbon neutral miners." This is unlikely to be achievable without significant changes to regional infrastructure. While the offsets from some of these companies are already driving a substantial part of the Gondwana Link reforestation project in Perth's bioregion, unless there are real efficiencies and moves toward alternative fuels, the carbon offsets for all their production will not be financially successful. There are many other regional resilience issues that face the Pilbara, including all the questions about local identity, indigenous issues, and regional governance. However, in terms of peak oil and climate change a bold vision for a diesel-free Pilbara can demonstrate that there is a long-term future for the region from which so much of the wealth of the country is presently derived. Every city in the world needs to develop a city-regional strategy for climate change and peak oil. Few seem to have begun to even think about their regions. Rural areas are generally in decline, though it is feasible to imagine how the post–peak oil world can enable rural areas to become more self sufficient and strengthen their economies around the production of biofuels, small-scale renewables, biopharmaceuticals and other biochemicals from plants, and the creation of more eco-villages.[26]

While each natural resource management region in Australia and in most developed parts of the world has in recent years been studied in great depth for the way in which agriculture, conservation, and water management can be better integrated, none appear to have addressed issues of peak oil and the decarbonization of the economy related to rural areas. The natural resource management regions have generally been established with a governance system and a set of grants to begin the management of valuable natural resources. The scope of natural resource management should be expanded to include oil vulnerability and climate change issues.

Another major rural and remote industry is tourism. It has become extremely dependent on cheap airfares and will not be sustainable in a peak oil world. This industry has been hit hard already, and, in a time of contraction in the economy, this is one sector that will be seen as nonessential in comparison to agriculture, forestry, and mining. More localized forms of tourism are going to have to be promoted as well as new technologies like airships, which can transport hundreds of people over eco-tourism sites in a slower but perhaps more sustainable way (they use one-tenth of the fuel). Airships can also be a highly efficient way of transporting heavy loads to remote areas; to mining camps, for example.

A major emphasis of the literature on peak oil suggests that the biggest rural and regional impact is going to be on agriculture. Certainly agriculture has become very dependent on diesel and should be a high priority for transitioning to biofuel.[27] The tension between growing crops for food and growing them for fuels will be an issue for agriculture and forestry to resolve over the next few decades. Tree crops that can assist agriculture as well as create opportunities for biofuels seem to be the kind of sustainability and resilience breakthrough that is required. In the dry wheatbelt of Western Australia a new kind of tree crop is emerging called oil mallee. This series of dryland eucalyptus species can grow in alleys between crops or pasture, they are deep rooted, enabling them to tackle the area's endemic salinity problems, the roots grow in large woody masses that store carbon for two hundred years providing a "carbon cash crop," the leaves have an oil that can be extracted and used in pharmaceuticals and in improving ethanol's performance in engines, and the branches when cut above the stump (which coppices annually) can be gasified to produce electricity or ethanol as well as charred for activated carbon.[28]

Biofuels will not be able to use food crops as their major resource or to clear forest for biofuel plantations where there is a net loss in greenhouse gases. Biofuels do, however, make sense if derived from ligno-cellulose sources and are not transported far; that is, they are particularly relevant to how they can be used by agriculture itself. Agriculture will need to adapt by growing its own biodiesel and switching to more efficient rail transport rather than trucks for long hauls. This transition will need assistance, yet in many agricultural areas like Australia and the U.S., subsidized diesel is preventing these opportunities from being explored. A crash program in diesel phase-out could change agricultural oil vulnerability in a five-year period. Much of the literature on biofuels shows that there will not be enough land for producing fuel that simply replaces what the world uses now, but there is enough for agriculture to produce for its purposes. Perhaps when ethanol from cellulosic material is better developed as a technology it will ensure there is a bigger role for biofuels.[29]

In Australia, to reduce cities' "foodmiles," horticultural precincts are being established immediately adjacent to cities. In these precincts lands with good soil are conserved in perpetuity for horticulture rather than always being seen as "market gardener's superannuation" from the next suburban subdivision. In these areas cities can then get serious about recycling wastewater for irrigation. In Perth the Carabooda Precinct will support the Water Corporation's investment in pipes to recycle treated sewage back into the production of tree and vegetable crops through injecting the groundwater. The British Colombia Agricultural Land Reserve has been set up for a similar purpose.

Biofuels can be produced that also generate carbon credits like oil mallee tree crops in Western Australia due to their deep roots and ability to coppice (grow back after cutting); these farm-forestry projects have multiple benefits for regional salinity and for generating local employment. (Credit: Timothy Beatley)

Eco-villages, as discussed in chapter 3, will help with food production and the green technologies of water harvesting, waste recycling, solar production, and biodiversity regeneration. These will be in areas away from the cores of cities, perhaps in horticultural precincts that could become eco-village precincts. The dense, mixed-use development of TODs can also include some of these green technologies but in less space-intensive ways. Eco-villages could help to reclaim a lot of outer and fringe development land that is not able to be incorporated into the dense corridors of the resilient city. But largely self-sufficient eco-villages on the fringes of cities will supplement the ecological processes of the city and reduce the need for oil-intensive agriculture.

Finding new and creative ways to connect local and regional farms and food producers/processors with local consumers can take many other forms of course: local farming cooperatives that collect and package and deliver food, farm-to-school programs that deliver locally produced food to schools (growing some food on school grounds, and working this into the school curriculum, as in the case of the Berkeley Edible Schoolyards program, is even better), and supporting and nurturing grocery stores and restaurants that buy and celebrate local food. In Portland, Oregon, the regional grocery chain New Seasons stocks about 30 percent local products, and uses special yellow tags to indicate these products. New Seasons carries beef, for example, from a cooperative of seventy ranchers in the region, who raise this beef naturally, without use of hormones, antibiotics, or GMO-feed.

Local restaurants could take more direct responsibility for nurturing and strengthening the local and regional producers that provide the ingredients for great cuisine. One such example can be found in Chicago. Here, the Frontera Farmer Foundation has been established by chef Rick Bayless, who runs the notable Chicago restaurant Frontera Grill, as a mechanism for providing financial assistance to small organic farmers serving the Chicago region. The foundation recently helped local farmers with a loan to cover the costs of buying new freezers, something necessary to allow them to store tomatoes and to sell them to local restaurants throughout the winter. As of 2006, several hundred thousand dollars had been raised through the sale of a specially made heirloom tomato salsa, the proceeds of which go exclusively to the farmer foundation.

In Western Australia a new household-based sustainability program Living Smart (see below) has produced a simple list of seasonal produce so that householders can check that they are buying in season and thus preventing the excessive food-miles associated with long-distance freight of "fresh" food.

Each step in producing slow, local food and fiber for a nearby city-region is a small symbol of hope that the city and its region can be resilient to a low oil future.

Regenerate Households and Neighborhoods

Virtually everyone lives or works in a building or house that will need to be retrofitted in some way for the coming petroleum transition. Many may live in traditional buildings that were built in a time of oil abundance (real or perceived) and natural gas made it easy to heat, cool, cook, wash, and use appliances without concern for the fossil fuels involved. And most neighborhoods are structured around the motor vehicle. Everyone will need to get involved in finding constructive solutions for their household and their neighborhood.

Every household has health and economic incentives to create a healthier, cleaner environment for themselves and their family. Perhaps therefore the most powerful program for change will come from household education programs where trained advisors come to people's homes and discuss the best options for saving money, increasing the value of their housing, and living better with more sustainable transport, power, heating/cooling, water, waste, and gardens. (This idea has been used in the TravelSmart program mentioned in chapter 5.)

Such programs are called community-based social marketing (CBSM). Canadian expert Doug McKenzie Mohr has collected evidence to show that people don't respond well to mass media campaigns or bursts of direct-mail publicity. Educationally sound and locally relevant material must be discussed with them one-on-one in their homes. When people see their options and choose to try new ways of transport or new ways of conserving energy, then the changes stick. Such lifestyle changes have been shown to make changes of 12 to 13 percent in how we use resources. The LivingSmart program, now being trialed in Perth, is helping households to reduce their energy, water, waste, and travel as an integrated package using eco-coaches. The 30,000-household experiment has shown some early spectacular results. From a cold call process the program is getting 80 percent of households interested in making changes to improve energy, water, waste, and travel efficiency at home. Fifty percent of the households contacted are signing up to ongoing coaching for special meter readings, advice on gardens, workshops, and home assessments. Unlike TravelSmart, where change occurs slowly and incrementally, the LivingSmart program is getting reports from households of instant and radical changes (replacing inefficient lights, ordering solar hot water systems, etc.). The program is on track for a 1.5 ton per household annual CO_2 reduction. This will save the households more than 10 percent in gas, electric, water, and petroleum bills.[30]

Neighborhood action groups designed to help households reduce environmental pollutants and oil consumption have been springing up across the world. In Australia over two hundred Climate Action Groups have emerged since the Al Gore's tour of Australia; they focus on the household level and also work to develop political agendas and lobby. They link through the Climate Action Network and a group called Lighter Footprints.

In the United States over nine thousand people across the country have joined the Eco Moms Alliance with branches in most major cities. This links the subculture dedicated to the "green mom," with blogs and Web sites like greenandcleanmom.blogspot.com, eco-chick.com, planetpatrol.info, treehugger.com, and grist.com. Women have played a major role in the environmental movement for many years, including the influence of Rachel Carson's *Silent Spring* and the leadership of women in campaigns a century ago to save the Palisades along the Hudson River and the sequoias in California, and the many women like Jane Jacobs and Meeky Blizzard who ran antifreeway campaigns. The Boston Consulting Group says women influence or control 80 percent of discretionary household purchases and hence become critical to the agenda for resilient cities.[31]

The potential use of the Web to link groups on climate change action is just beginning to be seen. Get Up was established in Australia to highlight major issues, and its fifty thousand members played a big role in the November 2007 election, which saw climate change as a major political focus. In the United States, Step It Up rallies, a day of climate-oriented rallies across the country, gathered massive support that could be seen when the full picture was put together on the Web.[32]

The human dimension to the resilient city will be critical to achieving the kinds of rapid change required in the next decade. Individuals (and communities) in our society lack the adequate sense in real time of how well we are doing—how much energy we are consuming, how many negative environmental and social impacts we are creating, how many opportunities we are missing to create cleaner richer lives and communities. Not only is it out of sight, we have no sense of how much we are using, and no feedback loops that might show us how and when we can reduce our consumption. Urban and building design might attempt to incorporate some of these feedback loops in very creative ways such as placing meters in visibly prominent locations, inspiring homeowners (and office workers) to see how much they can do to slow or stop the movement of the meter. The Center for Green Technology in Chicago has such a meter in its office, which sits in a highly visible location; it changes color and begins to make a sound when the office is using too much energy from its solar electric system. The Sixth Wave will need to provide more technology that can tap the need for households to audit and manage their own use of resources better.

The question which must eventually be faced is, What do we do on a neighborhood scale in our present urban structures? The next phase of the BASIX assessment process in New South Wales is METRIX, which will apply the same Web-based approach to neighborhood-scale developments and will then extend the approach to include transport, water sensitive design, and even affordable housing. The complexities of this have not yet been resolved. The same struggle is being experienced by LEED-ND, which is seeking to extend LEED rating in the United States to consider neighborhood sustainability issues. This is a big challenge as it is here that creative approaches to urban design can link the sustainable transport, solar buildings, and green infrastructure agendas. The LEED-ND pilot projects are underway, and these will be watched with interest. Other demonstration projects like Treasure Island in San Francisco, Mueller Airport in Austin, and North Port Quay in Perth, have the chance because of their scale to put together the whole package of transit-oriented, pedestrian-oriented, green buildings, closed cycle water and waste systems, and renewable power linked through a Smart Grid to electric vehicles.[33]

The big question is what do we do with the neighborhoods built in the 1950s in middle and outer suburbs that are now reaching the end of their life and are ready for redevelopment? They are usually locked into unsustainable patterns of transport with poorly designed buildings—often these areas are in population decline as their occupants age with lack of services and no other options for aged care or apartments for young people. The obvious next step in this process will be neighborhood-based planning to achieve regeneration of whole areas of suburbia. We call this greening the grayfields. (A grayfield is an underutilized area of land or real estate asset that needs regenerating.) If it is left to market processes it will occur one block at a time and will not be able to adapt to the resilient city agenda. Once poliycmakers and individual households see the advantage of becoming a more resilient community, the redevelopment process can proceed with whole neighborhoods refurbishing properties with the latest in green technology, infrastructure, and sustainable transport options. Planners in local government need to partner with sympathetic developers and consultants to deliver these more resilient neighborhoods through community-based design. Perhaps we need more "policy learning" and demonstrations before regulations and approvals processes can truly help in this area, but neighborhoods that want to be creative and help set this agenda will be very important in helping to show a process for greening the grayfields.[34]

Facilitate Localism

James H. Kunstler in the *Long Emergency* says that in response to peak oil "Our lives will become profoundly and intensely local."[35] Although localism will be a necessary response, it is important to note that this does not mean cities will no longer retain their regional and global functions. People will still need to travel to work and school, to theaters, and to shopping centers. People will still need to relate to the global economy and to global cultural events and global governance, which will require global travel. But it will not be as cheap and easy as in the heyday of cheap oil, and it will be increasingly taken over by more sustainable transport and more renewable fuels. The return to medieval villages or permaculture ruralized cities is unlikely and has serious potential risks.

Localism is, however, more likely to be the required modus operandi for the post–peak oil world, just as globalism was for the cheap oil era. To minimize travel for food, as we have mentioned, localities will need to explore more local production options such as "fifty mile menus" and community-supported agriculture (CSA). Opportunities for using local materials that do not need to be shipped and will contribute to the local economy should also be explored. Localism has other intangible benefits such as creating a stronger sense of place for residents. We suggest that governments establish an office of localism with a program to fund innovations in localism. Perhaps such a fund could be called the Beyond Oil Transition Fund and could be used to help fund demonstrations where

- businesses share their wastes as resources or work together to ensure local resources are used and reused as in the eco-efficiency agenda of chapter 4;
- local food linkages are made between peri-urban growers (and eco-villages) and urban communities to take direct supply of whatever is fresh as in the community-supported agriculture movement;
- local enterprises are facilitated based on local resources and talents as shown by Ernesto Sirolli and Michael Shuman (discussed in chapter 4);

- local tourism is marketed to local people; and
- local materials are sourced for buildings.

A number of inspirational examples exist of buildings and facilities that utilize a high degree of locally sourced and recycled materials in their construction. The Phillips Eco-Enterprise Center in Minneapolis is one such example, and in many ways serves as a prototype for the kind of post–peak oil economic development needed. The virtues of this model begin with its location and carry through to the ecological design and operation of the building and to the choice of building materials. Located on a brownfield site in the Phillips neighborhood, it's just a few minutes' walk from the Lake Street Station of the City's Hiawatha light rail line, and is also adjacent to a segment of the city's new Midtown Greenway bike and pedestrian trail. The Phillips Eco-Enterprise Center, run by the Green Institute, is home to interesting sets of green companies and businesses, and is credited with bringing 140 new jobs to this neighborhood. The building aspires to produce much of the energy it needs on-site. A large array of PV panels, visible to the surrounding community, is located on its rooftop, and extensive natural daylight is part of the building's design, including forty-eight solar-tracking skylights. These are special skylights estimated to bring in some ten times the natural light of a typical skylight. Other energy features include a geo-exchange heat pump system utilizing 120 sixty-foot deep wells (a closed-loop system taking advantage of the earth's forty-degree constant temperature). Also, connection with the native landscape of the region occurs through a green rooftop and most impressively a restored prairie adjacent to the facility. The prairie is periodically burned, and contains native prairie grasses and wildflowers. Perhaps most impressively, the structure utilizes a high degree of recycled materials, and materials derived within a relatively short distance of the building.[36]

The new community bank building in Astoria, Oregon, is one building that demonstrates the possibility of a new focus on uniqueness of place, and an emphasis on materials that are grown, produced, and processed locally. Designed by noted green architect Tom Bender, the resulting structure reflects an unusual effort at sensitively fitting in this structure to its larger community and landscape. As a form of organic architecture, it at once has a quite different look about it, overcoming the contemporary sameness of commercial architecture. Special emphasis

The Phillips Eco-Enterprise Center in Minneapolis (top) is a model for local resilience, show-ing many green building innovations, including a green roof (bottom) and use of daylighting through solar tracking skylights (next page, top). It is adjacent to a train station and on a bike-way (shown at a downtown stop; next page, bottom). (Credit: Timothy Beatley)

The Phillips Eco-Enterprise Center *continued*

has been placed on sourcing building materials locally, and this has happened in several ways. The onsite trees cut to make room for the building were milled and used for interior paneling and trim, outdoor wall shingles came from a local cedar shingle mill, cabinetry and interior partition wood also came from local sources, and the wood framing throughout the structure came from small local mills (including the use of "non-straight" woods that would otherwise not be commercially marketable). In the landscaping, salvaged plants were used — including reused native plants.[37]

Perhaps the most significant way to make localism come to life is through the slow food or local food movement. Shifting our food system away from long-distance oil-intensive food and toward sustainable local food will require action on many fronts, and there are already some hopeful models. Community-supported agriculture where local consumers buy shares in local farmers during the growing season, a kind of subscription farming, directly connecting with and supporting local producers, is one model and some communities have done much to promote and facilitate CSAs. In Madison, Wisconsin, for instance, there are twenty-five CSAs, and even an Association of CSAs to help and support them. There are now more than 1,500 CSAs in operation in the United States alone.

In many North American cities there is new interest in rethinking food — where it comes from, where and how it is grown, and new interest in local food. One measure of the interest in local and sustainable food systems is the existence of a local or state food policy council. Cities like Toronto and London in Canada have prepared comprehensive food strategies and sought to promote more reliance on sustainable local food, often couched in terms of the need to improve food security. The Community Food Security Coalition tracks the formation of such councils throughout North America, and reports that there are already seventy-seven local food policy councils throughout the country, and the number is growing. The number of operating farmers markets is another measure. The USDA reports an 18 percent rise in farmers markets (from 2000 to 2004), with a total of 4,385 in 2004.[38]

City governments could help in the formation and startup of new CSA farms, and could, through Community Food Policy Councils, help by supporting the host of other secondary but important elements of a more resilient food processing and delivery system: incubators to facilitate new food processing businesses, greenhouses for winter production, canning and freezing facilities, decentralized meat processing, and the

Astoria Bank building in Oregon demonstrates localism and green features. (Credit: Timothy Beatley)

many other elements of the local and regional food infrastructure that are often missing today.

A sustainable local and regional food system can be helped along in important ways by local planning and policy. Some localities are now mandating procurement of local food (e.g., Woodbury County, Iowa, has adopted a Local Food Purchasing Policy that requires purchasing local organic food from within one hundred miles), providing financial and technical assistance to local growers in converting to organic and more sustainable methods (e.g., Woodbury County provides a generous property tax rebate for local farmers willing to convert to organic production, for instance). Cities might help underwrite the purchasing of land and startup of new farms in the region, perhaps creating a small farms and farmer fund for this purpose.

There are a number of compelling examples of community food centers that can also help in transitioning to a local and regionally based food system. One of these, Growing Power, based in Milwaukee, Wisconsin, illustrates at once the possibilities of growing large amounts of food in a relatively compact urban area, making this nutritious food available and affordable to the less affluent residents of this city, and providing a facility in which urban youth learn about and directly participate in the growing of food. The brainchild of former professional basketball player Will Allen, the center consists of five greenhouses, where an amazing array of things are grown and produced, including Tilapia fish produced in a circular system where plants are fed fish wastes, and where water is circulated and cleansed in the process. In addition to the food center, Allen also operates his own hundred-acre organic farm as well as the Rainbow Farmers Cooperative, a network of organic farmers from throughout southeast Wisconsin. Other food centers incorporate community kitchens and provide space for new local food enterprises. Cooking and culinary classes and canning and freezing workshops that help residents appreciate and eat according to local seasons and seasonal farms are often part of this.

Localism can bring new life to cities as a renewed sense of place and local creativity is spawned. It does not need to be a reactive process to globalism but should be able to tap into the organic strengths of every city.

Use Approvals to Regulate for the Post-Oil Transition

"Most transit-oriented development in the U.S. is illegal" said G. B. Arrington, the father of Portland's rail revival and the head of Placemaking at the planning group Parsons Brinckerhoff. One of the biggest impediments to creating dense, mixed-use projects is zoning regulations that

Growing Power, based in Milwaukee, demonstrates how food can be produced in cities using cooperative ventures with the community. (Credit: Timothy Beatley)

continue to force separate uses and low-density development. The transition to resiliency will require changing the regulations we have so that they enable sustainability innovations to work.

Councils who need to approve urban developments will need to take in the whole project and judge it against a range of criteria and outcomes rather than against the rule books of planning. So, part of the new world is determining how to change our regulations to encourage the development (or, ideally, redevelopment) of carbon friendly, walkable, transit-accessible communities. Work has been done to this end by New Urbanists Andres Duany and Elizabeth Plater-Zyberck, who have produced SmartCode, a program designed to bring "zoning, subdivision regulations, urban design, and options for architectural standards into one compact document." This is a definite improvement over most standard subdivision codes, but this approach will not be sufficient until it requires much greater density and mixed use in its centers, with easy access to transit options (as outlined in chapter 5).

The regulatory challenges found in creating mixed-use, high-density communities are magnified for eco-villages since they also have to deal with energy, water, and waste. The Somerville Eco-Village in Perth, Australia, will have 120 households clustered around a small town on the urban fringe called Chidlow.[39] The development will be off the grid—sewage will be handled in compost toilets, electric power and water heating will come from solar PVs, and each structure will be designed and insulated for maximum energy efficiency. The plan calls for a dense, walkable pattern around a common garden space, leaving the majority of the site as native bush. The project has its own school and a range of small businesses that enable them to do most of the design and construction; use local recycled materials; develop water and waste management systems; manage energy systems; produce vegetables, fruit, olives, and wine locally; and rely on their own Internet and communications systems. It is mixed-use, relatively dense, does not rely on infrastructure links, and involves people who are already living on site. The response from public servants who assessed the project was paralysis and fear.

The project did not fit any of the rules and challenged every assumption about what was right and healthy (especially for public health officials who are generally stuck in the nineteenth century on issues to do with compost toilets and recycling of gray water). No zoning or set of guidelines for development fit such a project so the politicians had to override the statutory planners and give it approval. There was a lot of "policy learning" taking place. Having to override and battle for every regulatory change will not be feasible when we need such projects to be commonplace as we respond to peak oil and climate change.

A systematic review of regulations will show that at present across the world we subsidize oil consumption, whether it be through diesel rebates, fringe benefits taxes and salary packaging rules on cars and fuel, the sub-sidy on land development at the urban fringe (around eighty thousand dollars per block in most Australian cities and twice as much if off the urban front), as well as the subsidy given to road users in the form of road building grants. In the United States it has been estimated the subsidies to the fossil fuel industry are around $20 billion a year with global sub-sidies of $300 billion a year.[40] These are just the direct subsidies. The in-direct subsidies are in the form of regulations that require us to build car-dependent subdivisions and energy-inefficient buildings inadequate for the future.[41]

One way to enable the planning approvals system to be less encum-bered by unnecessary regulation is to focus more on outcomes, especially how we can use approvals as a way of achieving sustainability outcomes. So instead of regulating for a technology or type of fuel or material, the approvals of buildings and developments should be based on reductions in oil or carbon dioxide or water. As long as a developer or architect or householder can demonstrate that they are able to reduce their ecologi-cal footprint then they should be given approval. This was the genius in the New South Wales BASIX system as discussed in chapter 4. It is also the basis for the way TODs are being developed in Portland, Oregon. In-stead of approving one TOD project at a time and having the same po-litical fight every time over their "illegality," the Metro Regional Council now employs a master developer for each corridor that needs TODs. TODs are an outcome that everyone wants and are in every strategic plan, but they freeze sometimes due to local misunderstandings and in-adequate planning rules. The master developer is a consultant who comes back to the Metro with a detailed proposal for each of the TODs along the corridor, and all the approvals needed for the entire corridor are achieved together. Thus the strategic and statutory parts of planning are integrated—a solution to a growing problem in most cities.[42]

The local government approvals process modifies development through the local political process. This book suggests that from here on, every step in development needs to demonstrate how it will produce

- less need for a car, not more
- smaller ecological footprint (land, water, energy, waste) not big-ger—while improving the quality of life
- less need for fossil fuel power and more investment in renewable power

Regulation is also required at the national and international level, to phase out the excessive use of four-wheel drives and other gas guzzling cars with a clear phase-in program for electric hybrid cars. The same potential to switch to lower-fuel-consuming vehicles has been there for twenty years. The market was going to look after this ("trust us" the motor vehicle manufacturers said) but instead we got SUVs for the trip to the supermarket and a reversal of the gain in fuel efficiency caused by the regulations of the 1970s. Vehicles in the United States are now less efficient on average than they were with Henry Ford's Model T. We must regulate for motor vehicles to transition away from oil. Governments can begin by regulating for their own fleets. In 2007 the U.S. government required auto manufacturers to produce cars that get thirty-five miles per gallon by 2020. When he signed the bill, George Bush stated that it will help "address our oil vulnerabilities and dependency." This is an essential first step after decades of neglect. But it is not enough. We must guard against seeing fuel efficiency as the main outcome of energy policy; we need to renew our cities as well with complete resilient city plans. There is no simple technological solution to this issue.

Aviation is a special case. There seem to be limited opportunities for moving away from oil-powered planes. Although Richard Branson, owner of Virgin Airlines has committed to diverting all of his profits for the next ten years (beginning in 2007; approximately $3 billion) to develop renewable alternatives, including biofuel options for jets. Until alternative fuels become a viable option, the only solution it seems will be to allow gradual price increases to reduce unnecessary travel, to switch to fast trains for medium-distance journeys, and to do more and more by Internet conferencing (including family events). However, it would seem there would be a case to ensure that aviation had some priority on remaining fuel, though they too must see that growth in aviation, as it is still being planned, is not possible. This would also require some kind of regulation.[43]

Changing regulation is not a new topic in planning but it should now include the role of regulation as it relates to carbon markets that are being created to reduce greenhouse gases. The world's business communities are all looking to creative government to ensure these new regulations will facilitate a strong market. So far government has not done much to include transport oil use in these markets, and this must change. We cannot afford to depend solely on the market to handle the petroleum transition as it will continue to look for cheap and abundant supplies of oil from the Middle East. Since these supplies have peaked and the market will not demand reductions needed to lessen human impact on climate change, regulation is needed.

Regulation is not anti-market as the market must work to provide the products of a resilient city. But regulations can create these new markets by showing what the caps must be, where the dead ends are (like tar sands), where the external costs are too high, where development should no longer go (coal), and where it should go (renewables). We must now create markets for new fuels and for city (and rural) living in ways that just don't need fossil fuels. Carbon trading should be developed to include the carbon savings in transport and buildings by creating resilient city demonstrations. A new world is emerging where we must be much more clever in our markets, or our vulnerability to oil in both cities and rural regions will be exposed.

Conclusions: Cities of Fear or Cities of Hope?

Most advanced countries have developed highly complex scenarios for dealing with terrorism in the past five years. There are few such scenarios for dealing with oil and carbon vulnerability (or even for responding to natural disasters, in spite of recent extreme weather catastrophes).

The scenario we envision is that some cities will respond to the peak oil crisis in time and will adapt to avoid collapse. These cities will respond by cutting back substantially in demand for oil and any other transport fuel through a combination of city form and lifestyle change. This will be facilitated by sustainable transport modes, higher density, walkable, mixed-use communities, and community-based localism, together with new technologies for buildings including renewable energy, which will also be integrated into electric vehicles for transit through a Smart Grid. Other alternative fuels will fill some of the gap left by conventional oil decline. And some unconventional oil will be developed in deeper and remote areas. It will be inside our cities that the most change will happen as we respond to the new demands of peak oil and climate change.

This is only a sketch of the kind of future we could make. But it is a city of hope as it is imaginable with a series of steps we can take to get us underway, though none will be easy.

The first step is to create a clear plan. We need all our strategic analysts to take oil depletion and climate change seriously, to see what must be done in short-, medium-, and long-term scenarios for reductions in oil supplies. We need to see how we can reach the future of resiliency in a series of steps. If we cannot take the next steps we never reach the goal, fear takes over, and the paralysis begins to set in.

Some cities will not make the transition. They will be left waiting for the magic technology or the mystical market to sweep in with the solutions. As they push on with their present consumption patterns they will be hit by a series of shocks that are not hard to predict as the fuel begins to dry up. Those cities that are prepared with short-term contingencies, alternative transport availability, alternative fuel programs, household awareness programs, will be resilient. Those cities that are not ready will begin to crumble and fall apart, looking for someone to blame without looking in the mirror. People will leave and the problems of decline will set in. Finances to deal with the change will be limited and options will become less and less available as the processes of fear take hold of the financial institutions and the personal creativity of its citizens. The cities of fear can be scoffed at now by those who sit in comfort in the dying days of cheap oil. But they will not be good places in which to live when the lights of hope begin to go out.

References

Chapter 1: Urban Resilience

1. Atlanta was ranked eleventh in the nation in percentage of foreclosures. Realty-Trac.com, February 13, 2008; data on growth of inner city from William Lucy, University of Virginia, unpublished data.
2. Andrea Sarzynski, Marilyn A. Brown, Frank Southworth, "Shrinking the Carbon Footprint of Metropolitan America," Brookings Institution, May 29, 2008.
3. Jared Diamond, *Collapse: How Societies Choose to Fail or Succeed* (New York: Viking Books, 2005).
4. Caroline Ash, Barbara R. Jasny, Leslie Roberts, Richard Stone, and Andrew M. Sugden, "Reimagining Cities" *Science* special issue 319, no. 5864 (February 8, 2008): 739.
5. Worldwatch Institute, *State of the World 2007: Our Urban Future* (New York: W.W. Norton, 2007), www.citymayors.com/society/urban-population.html.
6. Peter Hall, *Cities in Civilization: Culture, Innovation and the Urban Order* (London: Widenfeld and Nicolson, 1998); Robert Friedel, *A Culture of Improvement: Technology and the Western Millenium* (Cambridge, MA: MIT Press, 2007); Lewis Mumford, *The City in History* (Hardmondsworth: Penguin Press, 1991); T. J. Gorringe, *A Theology of the Built Environment: Justice, Empowerment, Redemption* (Cambridge: Cambridge University Press, 2002), 140.
7. Ed Mazria, *Urban Land*, November/December 2007, 35.
8. Office of the Mayor, City of Seattle, seattle.gov/mayor/climate (February 15, 2008); www.clintonfoundation.org.
9. "Climate Link with Killer Cyclones Spurs Fierce Scientific Debate," Agence France-Presse (AFP), May 6, 2008.
10. On resilience to natural disasters see Mark Pelling, *The Vulnerability of Cities: Natural Disasters and Social Resilience* (London: Earthscan Publications, 2003); Larry Vale and Tom Campanella, *The Resilient City: How Modern Cities Recover from Disaster* (Oxford: Oxford University Press, 2005).
11. Brian Walker, David Salt, and Walter Reid, *Resilience Thinking: Sustaining Ecosystems and People in a Changing World* (Washington, D.C.: Island Press, 2006), 13; T. Wallington, R. Hobbes, and S. Moore, "Implications of Current Thinking for Biodiversity Conservation: A Review of Salient Issues," *Ecology and Society* 10(1):15 (2005).
12. This definition of sustainability for cities is from Peter Newman and Jeffery Kenworthy, *Sustainability and Cities* (Washington, D.C.: Island Press, 1999); in other books we have looked at the ecosystems and biodiversity that are part of city functions (see Peter Newman and Isabella Jennings, *Cities as Sustainable Ecosystems* (Washington, D.C.: Island Press, 2008); Timothy Beatley and Kristy Manning, *The Ecology of Place* (Washington, D.C.: Island Press, 1997).
13. Data on fuel use in cities are from J. Kenworthy, F. Laube, P. Newman, P. Barter, T. Raad, C. Poboon, and B. Guia, *An International Sourcebook of Automobile Dependence in Cities, 1960–1990* (Boulder: University Press of Colorado, 1999);

Peter Newman and Jeff Kenworthy, "Greening Urban Transport," *State of the World 2007: Our Urban Future,* Worldwatch Institute (New York: W.W. Norton, 2007). Reid Ewing, *Growing Cooler: The Evidence on Urban Development and Climate Change* (Washington, D.C.: Urban Land Institute, 2007).

14. M. Simmons in www.ArabianBusiness.com, February 28, 2008.

15. World Health Organizations fact sheet, "Use of the Air Quality Guidelines in Protecting Public Health: A Global Update." See www.who.int/mediacentre/factsheets/fs313/en/index.html.

16. Gregory Kats, "Greening America's Schools: Costs and Benefits," A Capital E Report, October, 2006.

17. See Peter Newman and Jeff Kenworthy, *Sustainability and Cities* (Washington, D.C.: Island Press, 1999); Howard Frumkin et al., *Urban Sprawl and Public Health* (Washington, D.C.: Island Press, 2002).

18. Mayer Hillman, *The Impact of Transport Policy on Children's Development* (London: Policy Studies Institute, 1999); G. C. Gee and D. T. Takeuchi, "Traffic Stress, Vehicular Burden and Well-Being: A Multi-Level Analysis," *Social Science & Medicine* 59(2, 2004):404–414; www.usgbc.org (Green Building Research) accessed February 2008. Surface Transportation Policy Project, "Driven to Spend: The Impact of Sprawl on Household TransportationExpenses," 2005. Barbara Lipman, *A Heavy Load: The Combined Housing and Transportation Burdens of Working Families* (Washington, D.C.: Center for Housing Policy, 2006).

19. On issues of place see Tim Beatley, *Native to Nowhere* (Washington, D.C.: Island Press, 2005) and Peter Newman and Isabella Jennings, *Cities as Sustainable Ecosystems* (Washington, D.C.: Island Press, 2008).

20. Municipal Arts Society, www.mas.org/climatechange, accessed February 2008.

21. Press release, The New Democratic Party (NDP) September 30, 2007. See www.ontariondp.com/hampton-proposes-clean-green-energy-plan.

22. Timothy Beatley, "Envisioning Solar Cities: Urban Futures Powered By Sustainable Energy," *Journal of Urban Technology* 14(2): 31–46 (2006).

23. Michael Shellenberger and Ted Norhaus, "The Death of Environmentalism," 2004 available at www.changethis.com.

24. Jane Jacobs, *Cities and the Wealth of Nations* (Harmondsworth: Penguin Press, 1984).

Chapter 2: Climate Change and Peak Oil

1. Larry Copeland and Paul Overberg, "Drivers cut back by 30B miles, 6-month drop biggest since '79–'80 shortages," *USA Today,* June 19, 2008.

2. In 1973 OPEC cut production of oil and placed an embargo on oil to the countries that supported Israel in its conflict with Syria and Egypt. These countries included the United States, its allies in western Europe, and Japan.

3. "U.N. Chief Seeks More Climate Change Leadership," *New York Times,* November 17, 2007.

4. See www.algore.com for further information about Al Gore's current projects, most notably, the Alliance for Climate Protection.

5. Executive Summary (full), HM Treasury Web site: www.hm-treasury.gov.uk/independent_reviews/stern_review_economics_climate_change/sternreview_summary.cfm.

6. IPCC, *Climate Change 2007, The IPCC Fourth Assessment Report*, IPCC (New York: United Nations, 2007); www.nobelprize.org/nobel_prizes/peace/laureates/2007.

7. Richard E. Benedick, *Ozone Diplomacy* (Cambridge, MA: Harvard University Press, 1991).

8. Kathy S. Law and Andreas Stohl, "Arctic Air Pollution: Origins and Impacts," *Science*, March 16, 2007.

9. Pew Center for Climate Change; United Nations Environment Programme, "Cities and Climate Change." See www.unep.org/urban_environment/issues/climate_change.asp.

10. Jonathan Norman, Heather L. MacLean and Christopher A. Kennedy, "Comparing High and Low Residential Density: Life-Cycle Analysis of Energy Use and Greenhouse Gas Emissions," *Journal of Urban Planning and Development* 132, 1 (March 2006): 10–21; Reid Ewing et al., *Growing Cooler: The Evidence of Urban Development and Climate Change* (Washington, D.C.: Urban Land Institute, 2007).

11. International Panel on Climate Change IPCC, *Climate Change 2007.* (Cambridge: Cambridge University Press, 2007) http://www.ipcc.ch/.

12. Association of the Study of Peak Oil and Gas (ASPO), www.peakoil.net.

13. J. Dowling, "Times Up for Petrol Says GM Chief," *Sydney Morning Herald*, January 15, 2008.

14. "Oil Scarcity Has Snuck Up on Us," ABC News (http://www.abc. net.au/news/stories/2008/ 01/30/2149569).

15. Russell Gold and Ann Davis, "Oil Officials See Limit Looming on Production," *Wall Street Journal*, November 19, 2007.

16. The Wall Street Journal blog, http://blogs.wsj.com/environmentalcapital/2008/02/07peak-oilers-put-money-where-mouths-are/.

17. George Monbiot, "Bottom of the Barrel—The World Is Running Out of Oil, So Why Do Politicians Refuse to Talk About It?" *The Guardian*, December 2, 2003.

18. Lester Brown, *Plan B* (New York: W.W. Norton, 2008); D. Cohen, Oil Drum, December 28, 2006.

19. Shaun Polczer, "Era of Cheap Energy Is Over," Says Buckee, *Calgary Herald*, May 10, 2007. See www.canada.com/calgaryherald/news/calgarybusiness/story.html?id=e6da17d6-eb3c-4a83-82a0-2858a739eb12&k=99612.

20. Matthew Simmons, Presentation to the First International Workshop on Oil Depletion, Association for the Study of Peak Oil, Uppsala University, May 23, 2002, available at www.peakoil.net.

21. Terry Tamminen, *Lives Per Gallon: The True Cost of Our Oil Addiction* (Washington, D.C.: Island Press, 2006).

22. M. J. Morita, K. Sedley, and J. Stern, *The New Economy of Oil: Impacts on Business, Geopolitics, and Society* (London: Royal Institute of International Affairs, 2001); International Energy Agency, "Resources to Reserves: Oil and Gas Technologies for the Energy Markets of the Future," 2005.

23. Michael Pacheco, "The Future of Ethanol," *Consumer Reports*, October 2006.

24. Data from Andrew McKillop, Sydney; Worldwatch Institute, *Vital Signs 2006–2007* (New York: W.W. Norton, 2006); "World's Cheapest Car Goes on Show." News.bbc.co.uk/2/hi/business/7180396.stm.

25. Overview of Natural Gas, see www.naturalgas.org; Productivity Commission, 2005.Review of National Competition Policy Reforms, Inquiry Report, Productivity Commission, Canberra.

26. Brian Fleay, "Natural Gas 'Magic Pudding' or Depleting Resource," ISTP, Murdoch University, 2002; Guy Caruso, "Short Term Natural Gas Outlook," Energy Information Administration, 2003; www.eia.doe.gov/neic/speeches/main2003.html.

27. Elizabeth Kolbert, "Unconventional Crude: Canada's Synthetic-Fuels Boom," *New Yorker*, November 12, 2007.

28. As reported by CBC, "Feds Allowing Tarsands to become 'Most Destructive Project on Earth': report," February 15, 2008, www.cbc.ca/canada/edmonton/story/2008/02/15/tarsands-report.html?ref=rss.

29. R. Miller, "Time to Debunk," *Oil and Gas Journal* (January 12, 2004), 10.

30. Michael Meacher, "Our Only Hope Lies in Forging a New Energy World Order," *Daily Telegraph*, June 26, 2006.

31. The bill deals primarily with four different categories of renewable fuel. Corn ethanol is capped at 15 billion gallons per year beginning in 2015. The remaining increase will be made up mostly by cellulosic biofuels. Green Car Congress, www.greencarcongress.com/2007/12/house-sends-ene.html.

32. Christopher Maag, "Ethanol's Issue: Getting Acquainted with Drivers," *New York Times*, December 15, 2007.

33. "The Ethanol Myth," *Consumer Reports*, October 2006, 19.

34. Worldwatch, "Biofuels for Transport," Wordwatch Paper, June 2006; Lester Brown, *Plan B*; Edith M. Lederer, "UN Says Soaring Prices Leave Poor Hungry," The Associated Press, February 13, 2008.

35. Juliet Eilperin, "Studies Say Clearing Land for Biofuels Will Aid Warming," *Washington Post*, February 8, 2008, A05; James Randerson, "Food crisis will take hold before climate change, warns chief scientist," *Guardian*, March 7, 2008, see www.guardian.co.uk/science/2008/mar/07/scienceofclimatechange.food.

Chapter 3: Four Scenarios for the Future of Cities

1. Alan E. Pisarksi, and Niels De Terra, "American and European Transportation Responses to the 1973–74 Oil Embargo," *Transportation* 4 (1975):291–312; Elsevier, 308.

2. Clifford Kraus, "Gas Prices Send Surge of Riders to Mass Transit," *New York Times*, May 10, 2008.

3. Alan E. Pisarski and Niels De Terra, Ibid., 311–312.

4. Jared Diamond, *Collapse: How Societies Choose to Fail or Succeed* (New York: Viking Books, 2005).

5. Jared Diamond, *Collapse: How Societies Choose to Fail or Succeed* (New York: Viking Books, 2005), 3.

6. Michael E. Smith, "Ancient Cities: Do They Hold Lessons for the Modern World?" Paper for the symposium, "The Relevance of American Archaeology: Intellectual and Practice-Based Contributions of Jeremy A. Sabloff," 73rd Annual Meeting of the Society for American Archaeology, Vancouver, British Columbia, March 26–30, 2008.

7. Jeff Goodell, "The Prophet of Climate Change: James Lovelock," *Rolling Stone*, www.rollingstone.com, November 1, 2007.

8. Lewis Mumford, *The City in History* (Harmondsworth: Penguin, 1961); Tim Beatley, *Planning for Coastal Resilience* (Charleston, SC: Coastal Services Center, unpublished).

9. J. Bronowski, *The Ascent of Man: A Personal View* (London: BBC Books, 1974); Paul Ehrlich and Ann Ehrlich, *Population, Resources, Environment* (San Francisco: Freeman, 1977); Ted Trainer, *Abandon Affluence* (London: Zed Books, 1985); Ted Trainer, *The Conserver Society: Alternatives for Sustainability* (London: Zed Books, 1995); and William Mollison, *Permaculture: A Designer's Manual* (Sydney: Tagari, 1988).

10. Les B. Magoon, "Are We Running Out of Oil?" U.S. Geological Survey, November 2000. See www.oilcrisis.com/magoon.

11. D. Lankshear and N. Cameron, "Peak Oil: A Christian Response," *Zadok Perspectives* 88 (2005):9–11, 10.

12. Adam Fenderson, "Peak Oil and Permaculture," *Energy Bulletin*, June 6, 2004, see www.energybulletin.net.

13. Michael Rose, director of the energy trading desk at Angus Jackson in Fort Lauderdale, Florida, as quoted in Clifford Krauss, "Supply Fears Push Oil to Triple Digits," *New York Times*, February 20, 2008.

14. Christopher B. Leinberger, "The Next Slum?" *Atlantic Monthly*, March 2008.

15. As reported by Michael Specter in "Big Foot," *New Yorker* February 25, 2008.

16. Jane Jacobs, *The Economy of Cities* (New York: Random House, 1969); Jane Jacobs, *Cities and the Wealth of Nations* (Harmondsworth: Penguin, 1984).

17. Peter Hall, *Cities of Tomorrow: An Intellectual History of Urban Planning and Design in the Twentieth Century* (Hoboken, NJ: John Wiley and Sons, 2002); Lewis Mumford, *The City in History* (Harmondsworth: Penguin, 1961); Jacques Ellul, *The Meaning of the City* (Grand Rapids, MI: Eerdmans, 1970).

18. Jared Diamond, *Guns, Germs and Steel: The Fates of Human Societies* (New York: W.W. Norton, 1999).

19. This is the term coined by groups such as deep ecologists who see hunter-gatherer societies as teaching cities how to be more natural. However, it rarely reaches policy other than in wilderness management.

20. T. Trainer, *The Conserver Society*; F. Gunther, "Fossil Energy and Food Security," *Energy and Environment* 12, 4 (2001): 253–275; D. Holmgren, *Permaculture: Principles and Pathways beyond Sustainability*, Holmgren Design Services, 2002; D. Holmgren, "Retrofitting the Suburbs for Sustainability," Energy Bulletin, March 30, 2005, www.energybulletin.net

21. Holmgren, "Retrofitting the Suburbs."

22. Mark Roseland, *Towards Sustainable Communities: Resources for Citizens and Their Governments* (Vancouver, BC: New Society Press, 2005) and Peter Newman and Jeff Kenworthy (1999).

23. Tim Flannery, *The Future Eaters* (New York: Grove Books, 1995).

24. These people are sometimes called "anarcho-primitivists," and their key notion to "rewild" society usually suggests a return to something akin to hunter-gatherer communities, see www.en.wikipedia.org/wiki/Anarcho-primitivism.

25. See Peter Newman and Isabella Jennings, *Cities as Sustainable Ecosystems* (Washington D.C.: Island Press, 2008).

26. Urban agriculture is covered in Darren Halweil and Danielle Nierenberg, "Farming the Cities" in *State of the World 2007*, Worldwatch (New York: W.W. Norton, 2007)

27. Peter Newman and Isabella Jennings, *Cities as Sustainable Ecosystems* (Washington, D.C.: Island Press, 2008); Timothy Beatley, *Native to Nowhere* (Washington, D.C.: Island Press, 2004).

28. Richard Heinberg, *The Oil Depletion Protocol: A Plan to Avert Oil Wars, Terrorism and Economic Collapse* (Vancouver, BC: New Society Press, 2006).

29. As reported by Nolan Finley, "Urban Farming May Well Hold the Key to the Future of Detroit," *Detroit News*, March 13, 2005.
30. Goodell, "The Prophet of Climate Change."
31. Jo Beall, Owen Crankshaw, and Susan Parnell, *Uniting a Divided City: Governance and Social Exclusion in Johannesburg* (London and Sterling: Earthscan, 2002).
32. Walker Wells of Global Green collected stories of affordable green housing in the United States. Global Green, *Blueprint for Greening Affordable Housing* (Washington, D.C.: Island Press, 2007).
33. Harvey Cox, *The Secular City: Secularization and Urbanization in Theological Perspective* (New York: Collier Books, 1990); David Harvey, *Social Justice and the City* (London: Edward Arnold, 1973); Bell, Crankshaw and Parnell, 2002, op cit.
34. Barbara Lipman, *A Heavy Load*; Wells, *Blueprint for Greening Affordable Housing*.
35. Center for Transit-Oriented Development and Center for Neighborhood Technology, "The Affordability Index: A New Tool for Measuring the True Affordability of a Housing Choice," released by the Brookings Institution Metropolitan Policy Program, January 2006; U.S. Department of Labor, Bureau of Labor Statistics, Consumer Expenditure Survey, 2006.
36. Peter Newman, "Lessons from Liverpool," *Planning and Administration* 1 (1986): 32–42.
37. Karlson Charlie Hargroves and Michael Harrison Smith, *The Natural Advantage of Nations* (London: Earthscan Publications, 2005).

Chapter 4: A Vision for Resilient Cities

1. Jan Scheurer, *Car Free Housing*, PhD Thesis ISTP, Murdoch University, www.sustainability.murdoch.edu.au; Jan Scheurer and Peter Newman, "Vauban: Integrating the Green and Brown Agenda," UN Global Review of Human Settlements, 2008, www.unep.org.
2. Isabelle de Pommereau, "New German Community Models Car-Free Living," *Christian Science Monitor*, December 20, 2006.
3. Environmental News Service, "Global Wind Map Shows Best Wind Farm Locations," May 17, 2005, see www.ens-newswire.com.
4. Alexis Madrigal, "DOE Report: Wind Could Power 20 Percent of US Grid by 2030," *Wired*, May 12, 2008; see also www.20percentwind.org for the full report.
5. Andrew Revkin, "Car-Free, Solar City in Gulf Could Set a New Standard for Green Design," *New York Times*, February 5, 2008.
6. Renewable Energy Information on Markets, Policy, Investment and Future Pathways by Eric Martinot, www.martinot.info/solarcities/daegu.htm (page last updated December 10, 2004).
7. Greenerbuildings.com, "Seattle, Los Angeles Announce Green Building Plans," *GreenerBuilding News*, February 28, 2008.
8. Cecilia M. Vega, "S.F. Moves to Greenest Building Codes in the U.S.," *San Francisco Chronicle*, March 20, 2008.
9. See www.greenhouse.gov.au/solarcities/ index.html.
10. Evelyn Schlatter, "Welcome to Smart Grid City, Colorado," *High Country News*, May 9, 2008.

11. See www.dpi.wa.gov.au/livingsmart.

12. See moscone.com/community/sustain.html.

13. Daniel Lerch, *Post Carbon Cities: Planning for Energy and Climate Uncertainty*, (Portland, OR: Post Carbon Institute, 2007).

14. David Biello, "Green Buildings May Be Cheapest Way to Slow Global Warming," *Scientific American*, March 17, 2008, see www.sciam.com.

15. Elizabeth Farrelly, "Attack of Common Sense Hits Planners," *Sydney Morning Herald*, April 26, 2005.

16. PowerLight press release, "Largest Zero Energy Home Community in Sacramento Region Opens," February 28, 2006, www.renewableenergyworld.com/rea/partner/story?id=44213.

17. See www.melbourne.vic.gov.au.

18. See www.multiplex.com.au.

19. See www.beltline.org; www.milliontrees.org; www.homedepotfoundation.org/suport_trees.html.

20. It is possible for a whole nation to go carbon neutral, and the costs are not beyond most countries; see Newman, Carbon Neutral submission to Garnaut Inquiry, 2008, www.garnautreview.org.au.

21. B. Williams, "Hopetoun Infrastructure Study," Perth: Landcorp, WA Government, 2008.

22. Andrea Sarzynski, Marilyn A. Brown, Frank Southworth, "Shrinking the Carbon Footprint of Metropolitan America," Brookings Institution, May 29, 2008.

23. City of Malmö, *Sustainable City of Tomorrow: Bo01-Experiences of a Swedish Housing Exposition* (Stockholm: Swedish Research Council for Environment, Agricultural Sciences and Spatial Planning, 2005).

24. Tim Beatley, *Native to Nowhere: Sustaining Home and Community in a Global Age* (Washington, D.C.: Island Press, 2005).

25. Mark Benedict and Ed MacMahon, *Green Infrastructure: Linking Landscapes and Communities* (Washington, D.C.: Island Press, 2006).

26. For blue green algae, see www.castoroil.in/reference/plant_oils/uses/fuel/sources/algae/biodiesel_algae.html; Bill McDonough, personal communication.

27. Josep Puig, "Energy Efficient Cities: Political Will, Capacity Building and Peoples' Participation. The Barcelona Solar Ordinance: A Case Study About How the Impossible Became Reality," in Peter Droege, ed., *Urban Energy Transition* (Amsterdam: Elsevier Publishers, 2008).

28. Thomas Starrs, "The SUV in Our Pantry," *Solar Today*, July/August 2005.

29. Marcia Caton Campbell, assistant professor, Department of Urban and Regional Planning, University of Wisconsin–Madison; Friends of Troy Gardens, www.troygardens.org; Madison Area Community Land Trust www.affordablehome.org.

30. See San Francisco Food Alliance, "San Francisco Collaborative Food System Assessment" San Francisco, 2005; Portland State University, "The Diggable City: Making Urban Agriculture a Planning Priority," Portland, Oregon, 2004.

31. Peter Newman and Jeff Kenworthy, 1999, ibid.; Herbert Girardet, *The Gaia Atlas of Cities: New Directions for Sustainable Urban Living* (London: Gaia Books, 1992); Newman and Jennings, 2008, ibid.

32. Paul Hawken, Amory Lovins, and Hunter Lovins, *Natural Capitalism: The Next Industrial Revolution* (London: Earthscan Publications, 1999).

33. See Newman and Jennings, 2008.

34. Clinton Climate Initiative best practices, www.c40cities.org/bestpractices/waste/toronto_organic.jsp.

35. Michael Shuman, *The Small-Mart Revolution: How Local Businesses Are Beating the Global Competition* (San Francisco: Berrett-Koehler Publishers, 2006); Ernesto Sirolli, *Ripples from the Zambezi: Passion, Entrepreneurship, and the Rebirth of Local Economies* (Vancouver, BC: New Society Publishers, 1999); www .sirolli.com.

36. Isabelle de Pommereau, "New German Community Models Car-Free Living," *Christian Science Monitor*, December 23, 2006.

37. Jan Scheurer and Peter Newman "Vauban: Integration of the Green and Brown Agendas," UN Global Review of Human Settlements, 2008.

38. T. Beatley and K. Manning, 1997, ibid.; T. Beatley, *Native to Nowhere*; P. Newman and I. Jennings, 2008, ibid.

39. Reid Ewing et al., *Growing Cooler: The Evidence on Urban Development and Climate Change* (Washington, D.C.: Urban Land Institute, 2007).

40. Robert Putnam, *Making Democracy Work: Civic Traditions of Modern Italy* (Princeton, NJ: Princeton Architectural Press, 1993).

Chapter 5: Hope for Resilient Cities

1. Claire Ferris-Lay, "Oil could reach $300 a barrel, says expert," www.arabian-business.com, February 28, 2008.

2. Peter Newman and Jeff Kenworthy, *Sustainability and Cities*, ibid. 3. U.S. EPA 2000, as reported in "Global Climate Change and Transportation Infrastructure: Lessons from the New York Area" by Rae Zimmerman (presented at Baked Apple conference, 1996); U.S. Department of Transportation, Bureau of Transportation Statistics, www.bts.gov/publications/transportation_statistics_annual_report/2006/ html.

3. Jane Jacobs, *Cities and the Wealth of Nations* (Harmondsworth: Penguin Press, 1984); L. Sandercock, *Cosmopolis II Mongrel Cities in the 21st Century* (London and New York: Continuum, 2003).

4. Brad Allenby and Jonathan Fink, "Toward Inherently Secure and Resilient Societies," *Science*, 309. no. 5737 (August 12, 2005): 1034–1036

5. Peter Newman and Jeff Kenworthy, "Greening Urban Transportation," in *State of the World 2007*, WorldWatch,(New York: W.W. Norton, 2007); J.R. Kenworthy, and F.B. Laube, *An International Sourcebook of Automobile Dependence in Cities, 1960–1990* (Boulder: University Press of Colorado, 1999).

6. C. Marchetti, "Anthropological Invariants in Travel Behaviours," *Technical Forecasting and Social Change* 47 (1, 1994): 75–78; SACTRA, "Trunk Roads and the Generation of Traffic," Department of Transport, London, UK, December 1994.

7. See Klauss C. Hass, "Bus or Light Rail: Making the Right Choice," *Environmental and Transport Planning*, 2e (Brighton, UK, 2004).

8. J. Michaelson, "Lessons from Paris," Making Places, June 2005, www.pps.org.

9. Peter Newman and Jeff Kenworthy 2007 in WorldWatch, op cit.

10. Arthur Lubow, "The Road to Curitiba," *New York Times Magazine*, May 20, 2007, see www.nytimes.com/2007/05/20/magazine/20Curitiba-t.html?pagewanted=1.

11. L. Fulton and L. Schipper, "Bus Systems for the Future," International Mayors Forum, Paris, IEA, OECD, 2002.

12. In the United States, with the passing of the Intermodal Surface Transportation Efficiency Act (ISTEA) in 1991, metropolitan planning organizations were given

the option to put some highway funds into transit-related projects. The most recent version is the Safe, Accountable, Flexible, Efficient Transportation Act: A Legacy for Users (SAFETEA-LU) passed in 2005.

13. P.A. Barter, J.R. Kenworthy, and F. Laube, "Lessons from Asia on Sustainable Urban Transport," in N. Low and B. Gleeson (eds.), *Making Urban Transport Sustainable* (Basingstoke UK: Palgrave-Macmillan, 2003).

14. Peter Newman and Jeff Kenworthy, "Urban Design to Reduce Automobile Dependence in Centers," *Opolis* 2 (1, 2006): 35–52.

15. Robert Cervero, "Transit Oriented Development in America: Experiences, Challenges and Prospects," Transportation Research Board, National Research Council, Washington DC; John Renne and J.S. Wells, "Transit Oriented Development: Developing a Strategy to Measure Success," TRB Research Results Digest, 294, Transportation Research Board, Washington D.C.; http://www.patrec.org/conferences/TODJuly2005/papers/.

16. Peter Calthorpe, *The Next American Metropolis Ecology, Community and the American Dream* (Princeton, NJ: Princeton University Press, 1993).

17. Ryan Falconer, "Living on the Edge," PhD Thesis, ISTP, Murdoch University, 2008.

18. Clifford Kraus, "Gas Prices Send Surge of Riders to Mass Transit," *New York Times*, May 10, 2008.

19. Denver Regional Council of Governments, DRCOG, 2004, Metro Vision Plan, Denver; www.greenprintdenver.org.

20. Peter Newman, "Transport Greenhouse Gases and Australian Suburbs" *Australian Planner* 43 (2, 2006): 6–7.

21. Jan Gehl, et al., *New City Life* (Copenhagen: The Danish Architectural Press, 2006).

22. Nancy Keats, "Building a Better Bike Lane," *Wall Street Journal*, May 4, 2007.

23. See www.vancouver-ecodensity.ca/.

24. Vukan Vuchic, *Urban Transit: Planning, Operations and Economics* (New York: John Wiley and Sons, 2005).

25. See Newman and Kenworthy, 1999. Peter Newman and Jeff Kenworthy, *Sustainability and Cities: Overcoming Automobile Dependence* (Washington, D.C.: Island Press, 1999).

26. Newman and Kenworthy, "The Transport Energy Trade-off: Fuel Efficient Traffic vs Fuel Efficient Cities," *Transportation Research Record*, 22A(3, 1998): 163–74.

27. Surface Transportation Policy Project, 1998. An analysis of the relationship between highway expansion and congestion in metropolitan areas.

28. S. Kearns, "Congestion Chargig Trials in London," European Transport Conference, Strasbourg, September 2006.

29. J. Eliasson and M. Beser, "The Stockholm congestion charging system," European Transport Conference, Strasbourg, September 2006.

30. Jan Gehl, *New City Life* (Copenhagen: Danish Architectural Press, 2006).

31. R. Gordon, "Boulevard of Dreams," September 8, 2005, www.sfgate.com.

32. David Burwell, "Way to Go: Three Simple Rules to Make Transportation a Positive Force in the Public Realm," *Making Places Bulletin*, June 2005.

33. Melissa Mean and Charlie Tims, *People Make Places: Growing the Public Life of Cities* (London: Demos, 2005); Andy Wiley Schwartz, "A Revolutionary Change in Transportation Planning: The Slow Road Movement," *New York Times*, July 10, 2006; Completestreets.org.

34. Jeremy Leggett, 2006, *Half Gone: Oil, Gas, Hot Air and the Global Energy Crisis* (London: Portobello Books, 2006).

35. USEPA, 2006; Laird et al., 2001.
36. Amory Lovins and D.R. Cramer, "Hypercars, Hydrogen, and the Automotive Transition," *International Journal of Vehicle Design* 35(1/2, 2004): 50–85, see www.rmi.org/.
37. USEPA, "Light Duty Automotive Technology and Fuel Economy Trends 1975–2006 (Ann Arbor, MI, 2006).
38. See blog entry, June 22, 2007, "Rollerblading to a PHEV Future" www.energysmart.wordpress.com/2007/06/22/rollerblading-to-a-phev-future/.
39. Michael Kinter-Meyer, Kevin Schneider, and Robert Pratt, "Impacts Assessment of Plug-In Hybrid Vehicles on Electric Utilities and Regional U.S. Power Grids, Part 1: Technical Analysis," Pacific Northwest National Laboratory, U.S. Department of Energy, DE-AC05-76RL01830.
40. Robert E. Lang and Dawn Dhavale, "America's Megapolitan Areas," *LandLines*, newsletter of the Lincoln Institute of Land Policy, July 2005; William Lucy and David Phillips, *Tomorrow's Cities, Tomorrow's Suburbs* (Chicago: Planners Press, 2007).
41. See America 2050.org and Neal Pierce's newsletter at citistates.com.
42. Department of Transport, personal communication; see Peter Newman, "Railways and Reurbanisation in Perth," in J. Williams and R. Stimson, eds., *Case Studies in Planning Success* (Amsterdam, Elsevier, 2001) and www.newmetrorail .wa.gov.au; D. Recondo, "Local Participatory Democracy in Latin America," Arusha Conference, December 2005; "Public Opinion and Transportation Priorities in SE Wisconsin," Regional Report, Public Policy Forum, 2006; Oregon, InterACT, Findings of the Transportation Priorities Project, 2003.

Chapter 6: Ten Strategic Steps toward a Resilient City

1. Climate Change and Energy Taskforce Report, city of Brisbane, 2007, www.brisbane.qld.gov.au/BCCWR/plans_and_strategies/documents/.
2. Richard Gilbert and Anthony Perl, *Transport Revolutions: Moving People and Freight without Oil* (London: Earthscan, 2008).
3. See www.C40cities.org.
4. Daniel Lerch, *Post Carbon Cities: Planning for Energy and Climate Uncertainty* (Portland, OR: Post Carbon Cities, 2007), postcarboncities.net/guidebook.
5. Andrea Sarzynski, Marilyn A. Brown, Frank Southworth, "Shrinking the Carbon Footprint of Metropolitan America," Brookings Institution, May 29, 2008.
6. Sally Paulin, *Community Voices: Creating Sustainable Spaces* (Perth: University of Western Australia Press, 2006) and www.21stcenturydialogue.com and the Tools for Community Planning series by Earthscan; Perth processes set out in J. Hartz-Karp and Peter Newman, "The Participative Route to Sustainability" in S. Paulin, ed. *Community Voices: Creating Sustainable Places* (Perth: University of Western Australia Press, 2006).
7. For policy learning see S. Owens, T. Raynor, and O. Bina, "New Agendas for Appraisal: Reflections on Theory, Practice, and Research," *Environment and Planning* A 36 (11, 2004): 1943–1959; and J. Pretty, "Participatory Learning for Sustainable Agriculture," *World Development* 23 (8, 1995): 1247–1263; for frame reflection see Donald Schon and Martin Rein, *Frame Reflection: Toward the Resoultion of Intractable Controversies* (Lanham, MD: Lexington Books, 1995);

George Lakoff, *Don't Think of an Elephant: Know your Values and Frame the Debate* (White River Junction, VT: Chelsea Green Publishers, 2004).

8. Bradbury and Raynor 2002, ibid.; for an example of the new engineering see Beatley with Newman, *Green Urbanism Down Under* (Washington, D.C.: Island Press, 2008).

9. This approach has been developed in depth by Bent Flyvbjerg "Making Sociology Matter: Phronetic Sociology as Public Sociology," in Michael Hviid Jacobsen, *Public Sociology* (Aalborg, Denmark: Aalborg University Press, 2008), 77–117; Steven Sampson, translator *Making Social Science Matter: Why Social Inquiry Fails and How It Can Succeed Again* (Cambridge: Cambridge University Press, 2007).

10. Jan Gehl et al., *New City Life* (Copenhagen: Danish Architectural Press, 2006).

11. www.uli.org/AM/template.cfm?Section=News&CONTENTID=107907& TEMPLATE=/CM/ContentDisplay.cfm.

12. Center for Transit Oriented Development and Reconnecting America, "Hidden in Plain Sight: Capturing the Demand for Housing Near Transit," 2004 (http://www.reconnectingamerica.org/html/TOD/).

13. See www.gehlarchitects.dk/.

14. Ransce Salan, "Kogarah Town Square—A Sustainable Development," ESD Strategist http://www.wsud.org/downloads/.

15. Cali Gorowitz, "TODs and Affordable Housing" report to Western Australian Government, PATREC, 2008, http://patrec.org/index.html; Hank Dittmar and Gloria Ohland, eds., *The New Transit Town* (Washington D.C.: Island Press, 2004).

16. Blake Dawson, "The New World of Value Transfer PPs," *Infrastructure, Policy, Finance and Investment*, May 2008.

17. William Lucy and David Phillips, *Tomorrow's Cities, Tomorrow's Suburbs* (Chicago: Planners Press, 2006); America 2050.org.

18. Todd Litman, "Understanding Smart Growth Savings: What We Know About Public Infrastructure and Service Cost Savings and How They Are Misrepresented by Critics," Victoria Transport Policy Institute, 2004.

19. R. Trubke, Peter Newman, and Jan Scheurer, "Assessing the Cost of Alternative Urban Development Paths in Australian Cities," PB-CUSP discussion paper, Curtin University, Fremantle, Western Australia.

20. Robert Burchell, Anthony Downs, Sahan Mukherji, Barbara McCann, *Sprawl Costs* (Washington, D.C.: Island Press, 2005). See Newman and Kenworthy, 1999.

21. Data from Peter Newman and Jeff Kenworthy, *Sustainability and Cities* (Washington, D.C.: Island Press, 1999).

22. The Free Congress Foundation, Conservatives for Mass Transit, Washington D.C., 2003.

23. Kintner Meyer et al, 2007, ibid.

24. Peter Newman and Isabella Jennings, *Cities as Sustainable Ecosystems* (Washington, DC: Island Press, 2008).

25. P. Newman, R. Armstrong, and N. McGrath, Pilbara Regional Sustainability Strategy, ISTP, Murdoch University, 2005.

26. Peter Newman, "The City and the Bush: Partnerships to Reverse Population Decline in Australia's Wheatbelt," *Australian Journal of Agricultural Research*, 56 (2005): 527–53.

27. Brian Fleay, *The Decline of the Age of Oil* (Sydney: Pluto Press, 1995); F. Gunther, "Fossil Energy and Food Security," *Energy and Environment* 12 (4, 2001): 253–275.

28. Erik Stanton Hicks, 2003, The Oil Mallee Project, Case Study for State Sustainability Strategy, www.sustainability.dpc.wa.gov.au; www.oilmallee.com.
29. WorldWatch, "Biofuels for Transport," WorldWatch Paper, June 2006.
30. See www.dpi.wa.gov.au/livingsmart.
31. Patricia Leigh Brown, "For 'EcoMoms,' Saving Earth Begins at Home," *New York Times*, February 16, 2008.
32. See www.getup.org.au.
33. Jerry Yudelson, *The Green Building Revolution* (Washington, D.C.: Island Press, 2008); See www.northportquay.com.au.
34. Portland's Master Developer concept is approaching the kind of process required.
35. James Howard Kunstler, *The Long Emergency* (New York: Grove Press, 2006).
36. See www.greeninstitute.org.
37. T. Bender, "Building Community Sustainability," Bank of Astoria, undated.
38. See www.ams.usda.gov.
39. See www.greenedge.org.
40. Ross Gelbspan, "The Climate Crisis and Carbon Trading, *Foreign Policy in Focus*, vol. 5, no. 30, 2000.
41. Mark Bachels, Jeff Kenworthy, Phillip Laird, and Peter Newman, *Back on Track: Rethinking Australian and New Zealand Transport* (Sydney: University of New South Wales Press, , 2001).
42. See www.metro-region.org/.
43. Michael Specter, Profiles "Branson's Luck," *New Yorker*, May 14, 2007, 114; On aviation sustainability in general see Richard Gilbert and Anthony Perl, *Transport Revolutions: Moving People and Freight without Oil* (London: Earthscan, 2008); on sea transport see Peter Hall, *Cities in Civilization* (Ukiah, CA: Orion Publishing, 2006); on airships see www.21stcenturyairships.com/.

Index